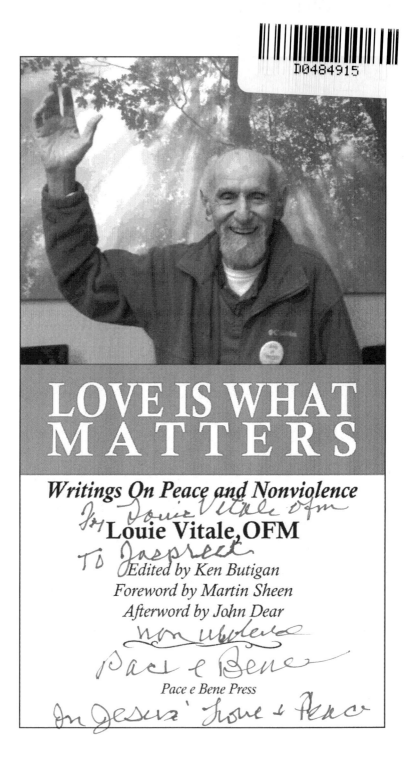

LOVE IS WHAT MATTERS

Writings On Peace and Nonviolence

Louie Vitale, OFM

Edited by Ken Butigan
Foreword by Martin Sheen
Afterword by John Dear

Pace e Bene Press

D0484915

[handwritten inscription:] For Louie Vitale ofm

To Jaspreet

non violence

Pace e Bene

In Jesus' Love & Peace

Love is What Matters: Writings on Peace and Nonviolence
Published by Pace e Bene Press.
To order individual or bulk copies,
visit: www.paceebene.org or call 510-268-8765.

Copyright © 2015 Pace e Bene
All rights reserved. No part of this publication may be reproduced, stored in a
retrieval system or transmitted in any form or by any means, electronic,
mechanical, photocopying, recording, or otherwise, without the prior permission
of the publisher.

Library of Congress Cataloging-in-Publication Data
Louie Vitale, OFM, 1932 -
Love is What Matters / Louie Vitale, OFM
ISBN-13: 978-0-9669783-6-0
ISBN-10: 0966978366

Library of Congress Control Number: 2015917104

Grateful acknowledgement is made to the following for permission to reprint
excerpts from the following copyrighted material.

"St. Francis's Conversion to the Nonviolent Life," *originally published as "St.
Francis's Conversion: From Violence to Wholeness,"* in Louie Vitale, in Ken Butigan,
Mary Litell, Louis Vitale, *Franciscan Nonviolence: Stories, Reflections, Principles,
Practices and Resources* (Pace e Bene Press, 2003).

"Reconciliation: The Bishop and the Mayor," in Louie Vitale, in Ken Butigan,
Mary Litell, Louis Vitale, *Franciscan Nonviolence: Stories, Reflections, Principles,
Practices and Resources* (Pace e Bene Press, 2003).

"Our Christian Calling: Care for Creation" originally published by Franciscan
Communications, July, 1990.

From *The Wolf*, (Pace e Bene quarterly publication), 1992-2007: "Guilty...and
Inspired!," "Jesus Weeps Over Los Angeles," "John Kavanaugh on the Las Vegas
Strip," "Sharing the Fruits of the Garden of Eden," "Ending Nuclear Testing --
Putting The Genie Back In The Bottle," "Ground Zero" on the Las Vegas Strip,"
"These Men Saved The World," "An Invasion Averted—A Step Back From
War," "Calling For A Response Of Nonviolence," "Nonviolence Comes of Age:
Hope for a New Millennium," "Exposing The Myth," "Review of James W
Douglass, *The Nonviolent Coming of God*," "Cesar Chavez: A Prophet of
Nonviolence," 'Elders Learn New Wisdom."

Cover photo by Paul Chinn/San Francisco Chronicle/Polaris
Design and layout: Ryan Hall
Interior photos by Jim Haber, Ken Butigan and others

Contents

Foreword by Martin Sheen   1
Introduction by Ken Butigan   2

Part One: My Journey to Peace
1. My Journey: An Introduction by Louie Vitale, OFM   11

Part Two: The Call of Saint Francis
Introduction to Part Two   19

2. Conversion to the Nonviolent Way   21
3. Making Peace with Creation   28
4. Making Peace Like Saint Francis   41

Part Three: To Jail for Peacemaking
Introduction to Part Three   47

Waging Peace from Jail (2002-2003)
5. Guilty...And Inspired!   49
6. Coming Full Circle: My Return to Nevada   51
7. Tears and Joy in Prison   55

Returning to Prison (2005-2006)
8. A New Monastery: Muscogee County Jail   56

Behind Prison Walls Again (2007-2008)
9. November 7, 2007   60
10. November 11, 2007   62
11. December 2007   64
12. March 2008   66
13. March 2008: Letter from Imperial Jail   68

Birthdays for a Prisoner (2010-2011)
14. Summer 2010   73

Photos of Fr. Louie Vitale Through the Years   76

Part Four: From War and Injustice to the Way of Nonviolence

Introduction to Part Four   83

15. Exposing the Myth   85
16. The Consequences of World War II   89
17. Elders Learn New Wisdom   91
18. Jesus Weeps Over Los Angeles   93
19. Dazzling Violence   97
20. Las Vegas Reflections   99
21. Sharing the Fruits of the Garden of Eden   101
22. Immigration and Nonviolence   103

Part Five: A New World of Nonviolence

Introduction to Part Five   107

23. Cesar Chavez: A Prophet of Nonviolence   109
24. Nonviolence Comes of Age   112
25. The Nonviolent Coming of God   115

Afterword by John Dear   117
About Pace e Bene   122
About Campaign Nonviolence   123
Biographies   127

Foreword

By Martin Sheen

Father Louie Vitale is the best follower of St. Francis of Assisi that I know. And he's the embodiment of everything Pope Francis is calling for. So it's wonderful to celebrate Fr. Louie's life with this collection of his writings. I hope they will inspire readers to join his lifelong campaign for peace and nonviolence.

I met Fr. Louie some thirty years ago at the Nevada Test Site, where I used to go with friends to protest the U.S. testing of nuclear weapons. Fr. Louie organized those protests and over the years, tens of thousands of us crossed the line for peace. Later I was arrested with Fr. Louie at the School of the Americas in Fort Benning, Georgia, to call for an end to the U.S. training of military death squads in Latin America. We've been together many times over the years--at peace actions in the Bay Area, with Catholic Worker and peace movement friends, and we even did a few benefit events together to raise funds for the poor and the homeless. I've also visited him many times over the years in various jails and prisons where he has been held for his peace protests. It was always a blessing for me to visit him.

I'm so glad our friends at Pace e Bene have brought together some of Fr. Louie's writings on peace and nonviolence as a way to celebrate the life of this great peacemaker. These writings give a glimpse into his Gospel life, his passion for peace and nonviolence, and his solidarity with the poor and creation. I hope these writings on peace and nonviolence, and his shining Gospel witness, will inspire more and more people to join Fr. Louie—and St. Francis and Pope Francis—in the global movement for peace and nonviolence to end poverty, war and environmental destruction, that we might welcome God's reign of peace on earth.

Thank you, Louie, for your peacemaking life and Gospel witness! You are a mighty blessing for us all. May we all strive to live up to your example.

Introduction

By Ken Butigan

In 2012 Franciscan Friar Louie Vitale received an honorary doctorate from the Catholic Theological Union in Chicago. The building was packed with students and their families who were celebrating their joyous graduation. The highlight of the event was the conferring of three honorary doctorates. Two scholarly gentlemen collected their award and delivered magisterial exhortations brimming with scholarly exegesis. Then it was Louie's turn. His presentation was short and to the point. "I've discovered in my life," he said, "that love is what matters in the end. And all I can say is: I love you! I love you! I love you! I love you!"

And then, with a final, rousing "I love you!" as he was waving his arms in an exuberant gesture of blessing, he sat down.

The crowd went wild.

For the three decades that I've known Louie, I have seen this love – and people's response to it – in countless situations. Louie is down-to-earth, earnest, passionate and deeply loving, and he exudes this spirit of care and compassion everywhere he goes. He is at home in the streets and in jail – where he has spent years serving time for nonviolent resistance to war and injustice – but also in the classroom, in nature, in his tiny hermitage, and at the dinner table with friends and strangers alike.

Louie has taken seriously the example of Saint Francis of Assisi and the way of Jesus.

A Franciscan priest who has sought to put into practice the peacemaking vision of Francis and Clare of Assisi, he served for years as the provincial of the Saint Barbara Province in the western United States. He was also co-founder of the Nevada Desert Experience – a spiritually-based movement that sought to end nuclear weapons testing at the Nevada Test Site – and Pace e

Bene Nonviolence Service, a training organization where we have been co-workers for over a quarter of a century. He also founded the Gubbio Project, a program that throws open the doors of a local church to the poor and homeless of San Francisco, California.

Louie has long been actively involved in a series of peace movements challenging his government's wars in Vietnam, Central America, Iraq, Afghanistan and many other parts of the world. He has spent long stints in prison for nonviolent resistance to war and torture. For thirteen years he was the pastor of St. Boniface Catholic Church in a low-income neighborhood in San Francisco, California, where he was actively involved with Religious Witness with Homeless People, an interfaith campaign challenging poverty and government policies of harassment against poor and homeless people.

Who is this latter-day St. Francis, and where did he come from?

The youngest of three siblings, Louie was born in Southern California in 1932 and grew up in a comfortable home in Pasadena. His father, who had founded a successful seafood company in Los Angeles after arriving as an immigrant from Sicily as a young man, expected Louie to follow in his footsteps. After graduating from college and a stint in the U.S. Air Force in the late 1950s, though, Louie stunned his father when he announced his decision not to go into the seafood business but, instead, to become a Franciscan.

Louie Vitale was enthralled with the life and work of Saint Francis. The son of a wealthy merchant born toward the end of the 12th century, Francis grew up steeped in the medieval vision of chivalric honor and romantic love. He went off to combat in a war between Assisi and a neighboring city-state. During one of the battles he was captured and spent a year as a prisoner of war.

After being ransomed by his father Francis underwent a profound conversion. In 1208 Francis took to heart the thoroughgoing demand of Matthew 19:21: Jesus' call to the rich young man to give everything away and follow him. Francis burned with the desire to imitate the poor and the crucified Jesus. He renounced his claims to his family's wealth and espoused "Lady Poverty" or "Holy Poverty" as his lifelong companion. A commitment to live fully dependent on the grace of God, Francis's vow of voluntary poverty was also an intuitive critique of the growing economic and social disparities of his age as it experienced the shift from rural to urban life, the rise of the merchant class, the coming end to feudalism and emergent monarchies and nation-states.

For Francis, God was the Most High who was Transcendent Goodness, a goodness lavished especially on the poor. To become voluntarily poor is to share the plight of the poor but also to share in the life of the God who gives everything. This God is worthy of praise and endless gratitude. Francis became a self-described "troubadour" — not a singer of earthly honor and romantic love, but a singer of the God who loves us with infinite mercy and tenderness. Gradually others were attracted by this vision. Originally contemplating becoming a monk, Francis set off in a new direction as an itinerant mendicant, preaching and witnessing to the life of God in Christ while remaining on the margins of society.

St. Francis vigorously counseled peace between warring city-states and between Christians and Muslims. His devotion to embodied peacemaking and nonviolent intervention is captured symbolically in the story of "the wolf of Gubbio," where Francis is said to have brokered a resolution between an Italian village and a wolf by meeting the needs of both sides. This is even more compellingly demonstrated in his sojourn to Egypt to visit with Malik-al-Kamil, the sultan of Egypt, during the fifth crusade in 1219. In the midst of wartime, he made his way across enemy lines to the sultan's base, where he sought to find an alternative to the catastrophe of war. With this innovative and historically verifiable adventure in peacemaking, Francis embodied Jesus' words to "love the enemy."

Like Francis, Louie Vitale experienced the dynamics of war. Louie did not serve in a hot war – his enlistment in the Air Force took place between the Korean and Vietnam conflicts – but he was actively conscripted in the Cold War struggle between the United States and the Soviet Union. This struggle came home to Louie in a clear and potentially catastrophic way during a routine mission that he and his crew were on one day along the U.S.-Canadian border. They received orders to shoot down an approaching aircraft determined by headquarters to be a Russian military jet crossing into U.S. airspace. Louie radioed his base three times for confirmation, and each time the order was reiterated. Finally, the crew decided to make a visual inspection. When they did, they saw an elderly, smiling woman waving to them. At the last moment they averted shooting down a commercial airliner. This incident contributed to growing qualms about remaining in the military. In contrast to the jet pilot's life, Louie felt increasingly drawn to religious life.

Louie became a Franciscan and later enrolled in a Ph.D. program in sociology at the University of California Los Angeles. In addition to his religious formation and his graduate studies, he was deeply impacted by the roiling social conflicts of the 1960s and the nonviolent social movements that were active at the time. Motivated by his Franciscan vision of the well-being of all, Louie plunged into a succession of nonviolent campaigns, including the draft resistance movement during the Vietnam War and the United Farm Workers' movement for justice for the migrant poor in California and Arizona. Eventually he worked for the rights of welfare mothers and helped found the U.S. Catholic Conference's Campaign for Human Development.

After completing his doctorate, Louie was transferred by the church to Nevada where, in 1970, he founded the Las Vegas Franciscan Center. He also became the pastor of a parish in a low-income neighborhood on the west side of Las Vegas. In the late 1970s, he was elected vice-provincial for his Franciscan province, and then succeeded the provincial when his superior was called to leadership of the order in Rome.

In the heady days following the Second Vatican Council (1962-1965), Louie became convinced that the work for peace and justice was central to the identity of Christians. This in itself was not unique. In the wake of Vatican II a growing number of Catholic clergy, women religious, and laity drew a similar conclusion and began to transform an insular church that had often supported social structures that reinforced injustice and war into a community prophetically seeking change. What set Louie and a relative handful of others apart was not their theological conversion but how they put it into practice. In his case, he marched and fasted with Cesar Chavez and the United Farm Workers, dramatically decried the U.S. war in Vietnam, and publicly stood with young men who burned their draft cards and defied conscription into the U.S. armed forces. He supported the nonviolent civil disobedience of Daniel and Phillip Berrigan and lent his support to a range of nonviolent social struggles. His years in Las Vegas motivated him to work with others to launch the Nevada Desert Experience, a campaign to end nuclear testing at the nearby Nevada Test Site. He also co-founded Pace e Bene Nonviolence Service, a small organization that continues today to teach and promote nonviolence through trainings, publications and public actions for peace (see www.paceebene.org) .

It has been a great privilege to work with Louie since I came to Pace e Bene in 1990. While we taught together in many settings—including a class at the Franciscan School of Theology in Berkeley, California that we offered over a dozen times, and numerous workshops—I was the real student, learning from him over and over again the power of following the vision of peace and nonviolence into action.

Nonviolent action benefits the world, even as it praises the God of Nonviolence who longs for the well-being of all. Louie's life and work clearly illuminate these truths.

In recent years Louie has followed this peacemaking path to Hiroshima, Cairo, and Tehran, as well as numerous cities and towns in the United States. In a series of speaking tours, he crisscrossed the country to spread the news about the power and possibility of peace and nonviolence. But some of his most powerful journeys have been into the prisons of his own nation. Here he has encountered profoundly inconsolable woundedness as well as a mysterious and transcendent sacredness.

For a world of justice and peace, Louie has been willing to cross again and again into the courts and the prison system as a kind of sacramental response to both the brokenness and the nonviolent potential that suffuses our world. The heart of this book is Louie's prison experience, and a handful of reflections that has flowed from this.

At the same time, this evidence of his own nonviolent faithfulness is nestled among a number of chapters about his great mentor, Saint Francis the Peacemaker, followed by chapters on a range of subjects crying out for nonviolent hope.

Penned on the road, at the margins, and even in jail, the reflections in this book offer a glimpse into the journey of this Franciscan pilgrim for peace and justice.

Part One begins with Louie's own life's journey as he reflects back on his time as a child through his decision to become a Franciscan and lifelong peacemaker.

Part Two reflects on the meaning of Saint Francis's life and work for us today. As a Franciscan, Louie has been imbued with the spirit of the peacemaker of Assisi and has, for half a century, devoted himself to living this spirit of transformation and healing.

Part Three presents a series of Louie's prison letters, written during long stints in jail for a series of nonviolent civil disobedience actions against torture and war. They help to convey

Louie's fundamental commitment to a world of justice, peace and reconciliation.

Part Four focuses on violence and the potential of nonviolence, in a series of short essays that first appeared in Pace e Bene's quarterly publication, The Wolf, beginning in the early 1990s.

Finally, Part Five highlights Louie's hope of nonviolence in our times.

Starting with Part Two I offer reflections at the beginning of each of these parts to provide some context for the writings that follow.

May Louie's insights from the past quarter century inspire you on your own journey to peace and nonviolence.

Pace e Bene is grateful for all who worked to make this collection a reality, including Veronica Pelicaric, Ryan Hall, John Dear, and Martin Sheen. We are also grateful for all the support Louie has received over the years for his journey of peacemaking including from his Franciscan community, the Franciscan Friars of the Province of Saint Barbara, Anne Symens-Bucher, Sherri Maurin, Laura Slattery, and many other family members and friends. We are especially thankful for the life and work of our brother, Louie, who has taught us in so many ways that "love is what matters.

PART ONE

MY JOURNEY TO PEACE

Lord, make me an instrument of Your peace. Where there is hatred, let me sow love; where there is injury, pardon; where there is doubt, faith; where there is despair, hope; where there is darkness, light; where there is sadness, joy.

O, Divine Master, grant that I may not so much seek to be consoled as to console; to be understood as to understand; to be loved as to love; For it is in giving that we receive; it is in pardoning that we are pardoned; it is in dying that we are born again to eternal life.

— The prayer of St. Francis of Assisi

1

My Journey: An Introduction

By Louie Vitale, OFM

I was born June 1, 1932 into an Italian Catholic family. Though I was baptized, my parents had some dissatisfaction with the local church and decided not to attend mass. I therefore initially missed out on the typical next steps: religious instruction culminating in first communion preceded by confession at the usual age of seven. About the time I turned 12, though, a close friend of my father convinced him, after much resistance, to attend a Catholic weekend retreat. My father was so impressed by the priest that when he came home, he announced that we were now going to Sunday mass every week.

Within a year I was in a Catholic military school run by Dominican Sisters. There my religious upbringing got a jump-start. I received instruction and made my first communion, confession and confirmation in short order.

I took to all of this with zeal. I was very impressed with a Dominican priest in long white robes. On top of this, there were many stories of priests who, during those World War II days, were like the martyrs of the early church—imprisoned in concentration camps, tortured and even put to death. To me, being a priest seemed like a very heroic lifestyle. But almost all my relatives were in business—mostly fish and liquor—so I presumed that would be my future life as well. Yet those heroes remained ever present to me, as did warriors like General Douglass MacArthur and General George Patton.

Entering high school, I strove to keep up with my studies and follow the faith, though this was challenging since now I had a car and had developed a wild streak with partying companions. Later I would come to learn that I had unconsciously followed in the footsteps of St. Francis, who also had been a carousing party-goer as a young man.

In my junior year I was talked into running for class president. When I lost I was humiliated, and I even blamed God for this humiliation. At the same time, I also saw it as some kind of sign from God. God was beginning to wake me up.

Until then, my major religious motivation was fear of sinning through human weakness and going to hell. Mass and confession could save my soul. But a new enthusiasm began to emerge. I approached a Jesuit campus chaplain—who had also been my high school principal--and told him of my interest in becoming a priest. He knew of my worldliness, and suggested that I finish college and complete my three-year obligation to the U.S. Air Force.

Once again hedonism won the day. I went back to the partying and jazz clubs, and I served my time in the Air Force. But the call never went away. A deep devotional side continued to develop. I made a retreat at a Franciscan retreat center in Indianapolis and, later, at the Abbey of Our Lady of Gethsemani. Here I was among contemplative Trappist monks, including the prolific spiritual writer Thomas Merton who had also turned from a profligate life to follow a mystical call.

The starkness of their vow of silence frightened me. The warmth and openness of the Franciscan center, though, attracted me. I picked up a vocation book at the center: "If you have a love of God, a desire to serve the poor as did Jesus, and if you have a sense of humor…" This spoke to me.

I signed up.

When I told my parents of what I had decided, my father was dismayed. When he said, "All this I will give to you…"—meaning the fish business—I remembered Jesus' temptation in the desert. I persevered in following the course. When I came to the end of my stint in the Air Force I faced three options: re-up with the Air Force, apply to Harvard for a business degree, or join the

Franciscans. The Holy Spirit did not leave me in confusion. I joyfully entered the Franciscan order.

As I learned more of St. Francis—his profligate years, his attraction to be a heroic knight, his experience of war, his year as a prisoner of war and his subsequent illness of body and spirit—today we would call this Post Traumatic Stress Disorder—I found myself following his path in a profound and transforming way.

My initial experience as a Franciscan was as a penitent. How could I regain good standing with God and achieve "sanctity" – from spiritual hobo to fervent disciple? The first two austere years were focused on submitting to discipline, putting on the Franciscan habit and taking up the religious life. I recall the fear coming back, fear of failing to live up to this way of life—the sins we might commit, not only of commission but also of omission. I was struck by St. Paul's confession, "The evil I would not do, I do; the good I would do, I do not."

But a strong conviction and love of this pathway of Jesus and Francis engaged me at a very deep level, compelling me to go on. After my novitiate I was ordained as a Catholic priest and took on the life-long commitment to poverty, chastity and obedience.

Major currents were sweeping through society and the church at this time. The Second Vatican Council and the new insights coming from scripture, liturgy, and church history—new understandings of the religious life and the role of bishops—were transforming the Roman Catholic Church. Most amazing and hopeful was the presence at the council of representative bishops from around the world, including Latin America, Africa, and Asia. Their engagement opened the global church to new forms of worship and new understandings of scripture and of God's message. The insights they brought powerfully informed the council's breakthrough document, "The Church in the Modern World." It proclaimed that the church was a church of the poor and the oppressed. The Spirit was moving within the poor to change history. Many of us experienced this as dramatically transformative. We Franciscans were blessed to have far-sighted mentors who already were immersed with the poor throughout the world, attempting to live St. Francis's charism for walking with the poor and for all creation.

Then came the powerful social movements of the sixties. By this time, I was out of seminary and sent to teach sociology at our college at San Luis Rey, and engaged in doctoral studies at UCLA. I also spent some time at Berkeley, where our theology school had located to be part of the Graduate Theological Union, an ecumenical community of seminaries, and to form connections with the University of California Berkeley (UCB), where the Free Speech movement had stoked student activism on campuses across the country. This was a heady and powerful atmosphere, and I got involved in the emerging Anti-Vietnam War.

I had come a long way from my U.S. Air Force days. I was now counseling draft resisters and joining public, nonviolent actions for peace. At the same time, I was fortunate, through the Franciscans, to get close to Cesar Chavez, the co-founder of the United Farm Workers, and to work with the migrant poor for their rights, including marching in a new kind of pilgrimage through California's Central Valley to the state capitol in Sacramento under the banner of our Lady of Guadalupe.

When the Vietnam War finally ended I was working in Las Vegas, Nevada with farm workers and for welfare mothers' rights. We did a sit-in on the famed Las Vegas Strip, temporarily halting traffic there.

About that time, I had a conversation with a journalist that had a profound impact on me. He said that, even though the Vietnam War was over, the nuclear arms race was heating up. As I reflected on this it became clear to me that one of the leading fronts of that titanic competition was the Nevada Test Site, only 65 miles north of Las Vegas. Hundreds of nuclear bombs had been detonated there for thirty years, and more were being

14

exploded on a regular basis still. Yet very few people in the United States knew this—or, if they did, seemed to care.

We reasoned that, if nuclear testing were stopped, the arms race itself would stop, because testing was a necessary step in the development, deployment, and maintenance of atomic arsenals.

So on the 800th anniversary of the birth of St. Francis—in 1982—the Franciscan community organized a new form of liturgy: a series of nonviolent vigils over 40 days at the Nevada Test Site culminating in a civil disobedience action in which several dozens of us were arrested at the gates of the facility on Good Friday—and a joyful welcoming of the resurrection at the test site on Easter morning.

Over the years we succeeded in influencing the establishment of a U.S. moratorium on testing that still holds, and contributed in our small way to the growing nonviolence movement.

Nevada Desert Experience has celebrated almost thirty years and is still going. It gave impetus to the birthing of Pace e Bene Nonviolence Service, which continues to provide resources and training in the spirituality and practice of active nonviolence.

It has been a great grace to be part of a growing movement for nonviolent change as we happily join the journey of the peacemaking Jesus and the band of Francis and Clare, Dorothy Day and Mahatma Gandhi, Martin Luther King, Jr. and Cesar Chavez, and so many others. In many tongues we celebrate the emergence of a new nonviolent order for justice, peace and the healing of the earth.

Hallelujah! Pace e Bene! Peace and Good to all!

Fr Louie, wrote this article on his life's journey while he was serving a six-month prison sentence for his prayerful, nonviolent protest action at the School of the Americas at Ft. Benning, GA in 2010.

PART TWO

THE CALL OF SAINT FRANCIS

It is no use walking anywhere to preach unless our walking is our preaching.

— St. Francis of Assisi

Lord make me an instrument of your peace. Where there is hatred, let me sow love; where there is injury, pardon; where there is doubt, faith; where there is despair, hope; where there is darkness, light; and where there is sadness, joy.

— St. Francis of Assisi

All the darkness in the world cannot extinguish the light of a single candle.

— St. Francis of Assisi

War is madness. Whereas God carries forward the work of creation, and we men and women are called to participate in his work, war destroys. It also ruins the most beautiful work of his hands: human beings. War ruins everything, even the bonds between brothers and sisters. War is irrational. Its only plan is to bring destruction.

— Pope Francis

Living the Vision of Saint Francis: Fr. Louie's Enduring Path

From his first years as a Franciscan, Fr. Louie has sought to fully grasp the significance of the life Saint Francis led and called others to follow. Most powerfully, this has moved him to "act his way into thinking" – to live the way Francis might if he were alive today, including following the journey of nonviolent love into the streets, into jail, and into a widening circle of compassion throughout the world. Each of these experiments in the Franciscan way has not only prompted him to deepen his commitment to the well-being of all but has also sharpened his understanding of St. Francis's example. The essays in this section that follows are the fruit of this long-term meditation on "the poor one of Assisi."

Here Fr. Louie first reflects on the origins of St. Francis's peacemaking. St. Francis was first a warrior, and Fr. Louie reflects on his experience of war and how it may have prompted his conversion. While many commentators over the centuries have underscored how having this kind of catastrophic experience sparked St. Francis's longing to undertake a spiritual life— something that echoed the conversion of many other saints before him—Fr. Louie was the first to reflect carefully on how the trauma of war itself not only played a definitive role in his spiritual awakening but also catalyzed his path of peacemaking. Specifically, he applied our contemporary insight into Post-Traumatic Stress Disorder and "survivor's guilt" to illuminate St. Francis's subsequent years of trauma and his own transformative breakthrough to following the God of Peace and becoming a peacemaker in his own time. Since this essay was published in 2003, a series of books have appeared that draws on and amplifies Fr. Louie's fresh insight.

Here also is an essay he was asked to write for Franciscan Communications in the early 1990s on St. Francis and his – and our – relationship with the earth. Although this chapter is now over two decades old, it's significance has deepened rather than diminished because of the insight it offers us today on the growing climate crisis.

Finally, in the chapter "Making Peace Like Saint Francis," Fr. Louie reflects on one of the last nonviolent actions Saint Francis engaged in, and its implications for us today. The titanic powers of the church and the city-state—religion and politics—were caught in a spiral of escalatory and retaliatory violence. Saint Francis upended this dynamic and created an alternative rooted in creativity and love, the lynchpins of nonviolence in his time—and in ours.

2

Conversion to the Nonviolent Life

*Once there was a great massacre in a war between the citizens of Perugia
and Assisi. Francis was captured along with many others, chained with
the rest of them, and endured the squalor of prison.*
— Francis of Assisi: Early Documents, Volume 2.

Nonviolence often arises in the context of violence. In his book,
Francis of Assisi, Arnaldo Fortini describes the barbaric attitude of
the era in which Francis lived. Warriors of that time wrote, "It is
good to see war tents spread out in the meadows, to hear the cry
of an attack, to look at the dead lying in trenches, pierced by the
stumps of bannered lances." No torture seemed too great as the
perpetrators and bystanders gloried in the blood and gore. They
rejoiced in battle and body count, which Fortini insists they saw as
giving joy to life. It also could bring power and riches.

At the time of Francis, civil wars existed in Assisi between the
rich and poor, the haves and the have-nots. These were wars
fought for power and economic gain. The new merchants fought
the nobility. But wars were also fought among rival city-states. In
1202 a very bloody war erupted between Assisi and Perugia.
Twenty year-old Francis marched off in a spirit of exhilaration
and glory. But the Assisians were overrun and beaten. Fortini
writes:

> "The sight of those killed on the field where the fighting
> took place was horrifying beyond words...All (the fields)
> were covered with the dead. 'How disfigured are the
> bodies on the field of battle, and how mutilated and
> broken the members.'...Assisi was appalled by the
> massacre... A great many of Assisi were taken prisoner....
> Among them was Francis... That battle with all its raw

21

ferocity and bloodthirsty pride, the sight of the dead, and the infinite grief made in Francis's warm and generous spirit a wound so deep that time never healed it."

After the battle of Collestrada, Francis was taken to Perugia and imprisoned. He was one of the fortunate ones. The archers and infantrymen were butchered, but the knights and those riding horses were held for ransom. Francis's prison was miserable, crowded and brutal. Francis made efforts to overcome the brutality and lift the spirits of his fellow-prisoners. Nevertheless, he succumbed to severe illness. Ultimately his father ransomed him. Francis had to suffer through a long convalescence, attended to by his loving mother. Over time he recovered his health. But Thomas of Celano notes: "From that day he began to regard himself as worthless and to hold in contempt what he had previously held as admirable and lovable."

Francis had not completely lost the hunger for battle and the longing for glory that was a part of his culture. Once again he set out to join a great knight, Walter of Brienne, in a campaign with the papal militia. He was even enticed into this crusade by a dream of his house filled with arms, shields and other implements of war. He saw this as a sign of success and future glory as he set out for Apulia. But a voice spoke to him and asked, "Who can do more good for you, the Lord or the servant?" The voice urged him to go back to his own land where he would be told what to do. Francis returned to Assisi, resumed some of his prodigal ways, but then encountered a leper, whom he kissed, and heard a voice from the cross calling him to rebuild the church.

Thus a very radical transformation began. Francis's eagerness to provide for the poor, and his desire to be in the company of lepers and outcasts moved him to an entirely different class in life. This was most dramatically illustrated when he went before the Bishop Guido and offered all his means, even all his clothes, to his father.

Francis took the words of the cross seriously and literally began to repair churches. He also joined in a very caring way with the poor and the lepers. Francis had made a dramatic social change. He had alienated himself from his family and his social grouping. In our contemporary usage, Francis had made a radical, preferential option for the poor.

The story of Francis's conversion from a life of pleasure, frivolity and excess to a devout follower of Christ has been told many times. In this chapter we are especially interested in one of the key consequences of this dramatic change: the powerful and transformative way Francis came to follow, and practice, the *nonviolence* of Christ.

Nonviolence emerges, as we have said, in the midst of violence. The more dramatic the violence, the stronger the temptation to respond in turn with violence. But horrific violence also can stimulate the opposite in some people. Some people, rather than desiring to retaliate, seek an alternative instead. They are motivated to experiment with active nonviolence. How might this have been true in the life of St. Francis?

Fortini describes the horrors of war and the impact this warfare had on Francis. Francis likely shed blood in the Perugia campaign. In the wake of this war and its brutality, Francis conceivably suffered from what today is described as Post-Traumatic Stress Disorder (PTSD). This term, though popularized during the Vietnam War, applies to veterans of all wars and to survivors of other traumatic events. While sufferers of Post-Traumatic Stress Disorder sometimes seek out new forms of violence and conflict, in many cases they seek to avoid conflict. They also demonstrate diminished interest or participation in activities they previously enjoyed; often they feel detached from others and withdraw from the external world. They experience recurring nightmares, sleeplessness, depression, hopelessness, irritation and anger. Francis experienced the trauma of war and bore many of the marks of a survivor of war. Dealing with anger was a continual challenge. In his later years he suffered from depression. He experienced sleeplessness, nightmares and dramatic dreams. He lost interest in things he had previously enjoyed, including spending time in nature.

Common to many people who endure war or imprisonment is "survivor's guilt." It is not improbable that Francis's exceptional concern for the poor was rooted, in part, in an abiding awareness that so many of the poor who fought with him in the war against Perugia had been slaughtered while he, the son of a rich merchant, had instead been held for ransom. An acute consciousness of this burden—the burden of being given back his life while others had not—may have played a role in his abandoning the privilege that had spared his life. This awareness may have provoked a dramatic reversal of his desire for riches, and led to its opposite: the longing to marry Lady Poverty and to live the fate of the poor himself. These are the qualities that made Francis a saint. His sanctity was spawned in a conscious struggle with the brutality of war and its aftermath.

Many who suffer from post-traumatic stress continue a life of violence. Some end their lives in prison or meet a violent death. Some recover, some do not. The severity of the trauma is often a predictor. For Francis the conditions were, as Fortini suggests, extremely severe. But Francis had the unique grace to turn these disorders into a path toward holiness.

One of the most important ways to calm great stress is through meditation. Francis entered caves in the hills and drew closer to God. He re-engaged with nature. He gave himself in service to others which can often be remarkably curative. He sought to re-write the "script," as when he went before the Sultan with only a cross. He overcame his fear of robbers and wolves. He treated all—especially those with leprosy, who had been segregated from the larger society—with deep respect, cherishing each one as bearing the face of Christ. In these and many other ways he overcame the violence within himself and healed the trauma. His close relationships with the Brothers and with Clare brought him into a new and profound sense of community.

These traits mark the way of nonviolence. They lead to a deep transformation of heart and to what Martin Luther King, Jr. referred to as the "Beloved Community." Francis's deep appreciation of every person led him to see no one as an enemy. He preferred to welcome enemies into his midst and turn them into friends.

Although Francis started out as a combatant, he became a conscientious objector. He withdrew from his commitment to the Crusade of Walter of Brienne and embodied a commitment of disarmament by carrying a cross, not a sword.

Moreover, he encouraged others to put down the sword. As Former Minister General of the Friars Minor Herman Schaluck noted, "He forbade all of his followers to carry weapons. As a result, it became difficult for some feudal lords to muster an army together, as there were so many Secular Franciscans who refused to carry arms. This simple demand by Francis led to the collapse of the feudal system in Europe." As Brother Herman suggests, Francis is an apt model in our own day. He once saw war as a road to glory, but eventually came to see its human devastation. Such awareness is acutely needed in today's world of carpet-bombing, smart bombs, terrorism, drone attacks, and nuclear weapons. As Brother Herman suggests, there are indications that Francis helped bring about the abolition of war in certain parts of Europe during the Middle Ages.

Ultimately, we are speaking of a deep religious conversion. Francis transcended the extreme violence of his times. He had been touched and transformed by the compassion of God. He recognized that there is woundedness *and* sacredness in every person and in all of creation, and began to love and respect everyone.

This is the starting point of nonviolence. The transforming power of nonviolence begins and ends with an awareness of the presence of God in everyone. It is this presence that breaks the spiral of violence. The Spirit of our unifying God is present when conflict is resolved, when the script of violence is rewritten to embrace the sacredness of all parties and when creativity is used to break the cycle of retaliation. Moving from his woundedness, Francis undergoes a deep conversion from the drive of violence to loving nonviolence. He came to see that an all-loving God is a God of compassion, and that human beings are meant to love and be loved, radically and totally. This dynamic challenges us to overcome the divisions that separate us and to discover the underlying sacredness that unites us, and to make peace.

Francis comes, finally, to understand his true vocation, the calling to love everyone as God has loved us. In practical terms this means resisting the tendency of violence to divide the world into various enemy camps. Practitioners of nonviolence seek to become their truest selves by loving all beings, especially their enemies. In verse 38 of his *Later Admonition and Exhortation to the Brothers and Sisters of Penance* Francis urges us to follow the Gospel: "We must love our enemies and do good to those who hate us."

In verse 23 of his *Testament,* Francis tells us that "The Lord revealed to me that we should greet one another by saying: 'May the Lord give you peace.'" Bonaventure recalls: "At the beginning and end of every sermon he announced peace; in every greeting he wished for peace. Francis instructed his brothers, as they entered someone's house, to say, "Peace to this house." He wanted us to speak words of peace and, more importantly, to become agents of this peace in the world.

Historian and theologian Joseph Chinnici, O.F.M. asks the question: "Why does Francis use these greetings which, historically speaking, were unusual and uncommon at that time?" Chinnici suggests that Francis's greetings of peace comprise a social act. They are a call to overcome the dominant violence of the times and the system of dominance that fosters and promotes violence. To seek such peace is a communal act; it is active nonviolence. It addresses the structure of violence, as well as the political and economic systems that separate people into warring parties. Chinnici writes that the central thrust of Francis's life pursuit was to overcome violence with a new call for peace and nonviolence. And if we, like Francis, address and transform violence, we become more like Christ.

Through his own experience of violence, Francis identified with the one who overcame violence. He identified with the one who told Peter to put down the sword and who healed the servant's ear. He identified with the one who prayed from the cross, "Father forgive them for they know not what they do." Francis's stigmata was a sign of his total identification with the nonviolent Christ, a sign of his full conversion from warrior to peacemaker.

The greeting of Christ after his resurrection was "Peace be with you." Francis took that message to the world of his time. He wanted peace for all people and all creation. This remains the challenge for our times. To do this, as Father Chinnici suggests, we "need armies of brothers and sisters who manifest peace." All of us can join Francis's transformation and become people of nonviolence who carry on his work for peace.

3

Making Peace With Creation

Born and raised in Southern California, I remember what that land of sunshine and crystal air was like before smog. As a child I ran on clean beaches and dove into the waves. The pounding surf gave me a sense of God. And in the nearby mountains I would look up at the tall fir trees and could not see their tops. This natural cathedral also made me think of God. To me there was no grander place in the world than beautiful California.

As the years passed, I experienced a genuine sense of loss as the natural beauty slowly disappeared. I recall the scenes of my childhood as one might remember a friend who died. Oil spills suffocate marine life and shroud the beaches with tar. Raw sewage contaminates the surviving fish and infects bathers with skin and eye irritations. On land, industrial chemicals and human and animal wastes reduce the already dwindling ground supply of drinking water. In the air, ozone pollution has exceeded the government standard for air quality control on almost one out of every two days for the last decade. Wildlife disappears as wetlands dry up and forests turn a somber brown. The cathedrals of nature have been desecrated and the signs of God's presence disfigured with pollution's graffiti.

"In the beginning, when God created the heavens and the earth... God saw that it was good" (Genesis 1:1,10). Creation's Creator set all things in plentiful balance: night and day, winter and summer, dry land and oceans: "Let the earth bring forth vegetation... Let the water teem with an abundance of living creatures" (Genesis 1:11,20). It was all very good, self-replenishing, sufficient and beautiful. Then God created humanity to "fill the earth and subdue it. Have dominion over the fish...the birds...and all living things." When speaking of "dominion," the author of Genesis had in mind some of the good kings of Israel who shepherded God's people, imaging God's own loving concern for all creation. But in general, we humans increasingly misinterpreted the meaning of "dominion" as domination and exploitation instead of stewardship.

As humanity emptied the earth of its resources, God admonished them again: "Do not damage the land or the sea or the trees..." (Rev 7:3). "Was it not enough for you to graze on the best pasture, that you had to trample the rest of your pastures with your feet? Was it not enough for you to drink the clearest water, that you had to foul the remainder with your feet?" (Ezekiel 34:18).

Like Adam and Eve, we have misused the fruits of creation, turning God's garden into a wasteland. Like Cain we have killed our brother, Abel a thousand times over as we decimate irreplaceable species, destroy forest upon forest, litter the world with plastic.

Saint Francis

Saint Francis of Assisi heard the message of God's goodness for creation's interdependence and humanity's responsibility toward it. He serves as a patron of ecology for our time. Professor Lynn White called St. Francis the greatest spiritual revolutionary in Western history. In 1969 he proposed Francis as the patron of ecology. Ten years later Pope John Paul II made this official. In his first letter on the environment, in 1990, the Pope presented Francis as our model: "Francis...offers Christians an example of genuine and deep respect for the integrity of creation."

Why, in the midst of modern industrial pollution, holes in the ozone layer, global warming and nuclear radiation, do we look to a person of the thirteenth century for guidance?

Francis loved nature. He was one with the world around him. He found such joy in nature that he would burst out in song. He saw God radiating in all of creation. Francis pointed out how useful nature is. It offers pure water to drink, air to breath and fire to light the night. Mother earth to arrange the seasons to sustain and govern us. Centuries before the environment became a concern, Francis saw human beings abuse nature. In what might be the first ecological statement outside of the Bible, Francis admonished the people around him, as reported in the *Legend of Perusia*, "These creatures minister to our needs every day; without them we could not live and through them the human race greatly offends the Creator every time we fail to appreciate so great a blessing."

Toward the end of his life, Francis wanted to send a message to the world about creation. Although almost blind, he composed the famous "Canticle of the Creatures." In the Canticle Francis called all living beings, even the elements of the universe, brother or sister:

Most high, all powerful, all good Lord!
All praise is yours, all glory, all honor
And all blessing.

To you, alone, Most High, do they belong.
No mortals are worthy
To pronounce your name.

All praise be yours, my Lord, through all that you have made,
And first my lord Brother Sun,
Who brings the day; and light you give to us through him.
How beautiful is he, how radiant in all his splendor!
Of you, Most High, he bears the likeness.

All praise be yours, my Lord, through Sister Moon and Stars:
In the heavens you have made them bright and precious and fair.

All praise be yours, my Lord, through Brothers Wind and Air,
And fair and stormy, all the weather's moods,
By which you cherish all that you have made.

All praise be yours, my Lord, through Sister Water,
So useful, lowly, precious and pure.

All praise be yours, my Lord, through Brother Fire,
Through whom you brighten up the night.
How beautiful is he! Full of power and strength.

All praise be yours, my Lord, through Sister Earth, our mother,
Who feeds us in her sovereignty and produces
Various fruits with colored flowers and herbs.

All praise be yours, my Lord, through those who grant pardon,
For love of you; through those who endure sickness and trial.

Happy those who endure in peace,
By you, Most High, they will be crowned.

All praise be yours, my Lord, through Sister Death,
From whose embrace no mortal can escape.
Woe to those who die in mortal sin!
Happy those She finds doing your will!
The second death can do no harm to them.

Praise and bless the Lord, and give him thanks,
And serve him with great humility.

In the Canticle, Francis expressed what today we call "Deep Ecology". Nature and created beings exist in their own right and not just because they are useful to us. All beings have the right to reach their fullness and to be guaranteed their natural habitat. Created by God, they are of great worth and give glory to God, even if we humans did not exist.

Francis composed his Canticle in the popular Italian of the day rather than in the more formal Latin. He wanted ordinary people to hear his message. He sent friars as troubadours to spread its message throughout the world. Franciscans continue to fulfill this mandate. They bring the message of peace and concern for creation to people in churches, schools, councils and congresses.

Peoples of all faiths look to Francis in the present environmental crisis. Many are learning with Francis that God's Word calls us to be stewards of creation. At the root of this crisis is the question of faith: Whose world is this? How do we humans relate, not only to God and to each other, but to the natural world as well?

The Myth Of Progress

What happened between the time and spirit of Saint Francis and today? Our alienation from nature, from fraternal solidarity and from God has spread like a disease. Francis saw our alienation from nature as a sign of sin. He strove to restore the harmony of the Garden of Eden, where the needs of all were met. Since then many have pursued that same goal, but the means we have chosen to bring about progress have often brought even more havoc to nature and humanity.

Twenty years ago I moved from Los Angeles to Las Vegas, which was then a rather small city. The surrounding desert and mountains still recalled God's creation, but not for long. I remember hearing the first radio report about smog in the city. Today Las Vegas is a boomtown, the fastest growing city in the fastest growing state in the nation. A weekend escape, it's big, fast, and fascinating, the epitome of "progress."

But the city's commercial success depends on an extravagant waste of energy and water. The trade off for the 24-hour glitter includes pollution and the faults attributed to Adam, Cain and Esau: misused resources, greed, unbridled consumption and the craving for instantaneous pleasure. Like Sodom and Gomorrah, we wonder how long cities like Las Vegas can remain livable. Perhaps Las Vegas serves as a warning, a microcosm of the world.

But there is more.

Sixty miles north of Las Vegas is the Nevada Test Site. From 1951 to 1992, virtually all of the United States' nuclear weapons were tested there—first above ground, and then underground after the passage of the Partial Test Ban Treaty in 1963. Those of us who lived in Las Vegas during those years would hear warnings on the radio ahead of many of the large megaton explosions in the desert, so that people could come down from high-rise buildings and up from the mines. "Today there will be a nuclear blast with a range of 20 to 150 kilotons," they would announce. Most of the detonations represented a destructive force several times worse than the atomic bombs that reduced the entire cities of Hiroshima and Nagasaki to ashes. The tremors were monitored like earthquakes hundreds of miles away where they registered 5 and 6 on the Richter scale. Sensitive instruments measured how much radiation leaked into the atmosphere. And what about the earth below us and our water system? No one knows just how contaminated they became.

In 1982, dozens of us marked the 800th anniversary of the birth of Saint Francis by praying and vigiling at the gates of the Nevada Test Site during the forty days of Lent. For decades we have continued this witness as the *Nevada Desert Experience*. With thousands of people making a pilgrimage of peace to the Nevada Test Site over the last 30 years, we contributed to a global movement to establish the Comprehensive Test Ban Treaty

(CTBT) that was promulgated in the early 1990s and approved by over 150 nations. Although the United States has not signed the CTBT, it has abided by it for over 20 years.

Before the CTBT was established, we engaged with others around the world in a fast to end nuclear weapons testing. We camped in the scrub-covered desert just outside the Nevada Test Site. One morning an underground test was conducted. We stood with our peace signs held high and bowed our heads in prayer. A wave of shame overwhelmed me as I thought of what violence we were doing to Mother Earth and to the air around us.

The government later admitted that radioactive gasses had leaked into the atmosphere. How many Nevada Test Site employees were affected? How many workers' spouses would eventually be added to the number of Nevada Test Site widows? Shouldn't this test site have been evacuated the way Chernobyl in Russia was to protect workers and residents? I must confess some panic at the thought that my own body was contaminated with radiation.

Nuclear weapons and waste are key tests of our humanity today. Are we ready to deal with the specter of extinction through nuclear radiation? Are we willing to risk the consequences of a nuclear confrontation—a nuclear winter brought on by dust and debris so enshrouding the globe that it cuts off the sun's warmth—till only microscopic forms of life survive?

Since Francis's time modern technology has accelerated beyond imagination, but not without costs. Until recently, factories symbolized growth and development. We wanted goods—bigger, faster, in all sizes and colors, with all the gadgets, prepackaged and ready. We exploited natural resources without limit anywhere in the world. We drilled oil until it glutted the market and covered our shores like a pall.

But nobody was keeping score. No one looked to see if we would ever run out of our natural resources. No one asked about the consequences to our water supply or farmlands or rain forests.

No one questioned whether or not the thousands of metal drums disposed of at sea would ever rust. No one considered the impact upon future generations.

It never crossed our minds that there could be too much progress. We wanted big cities, big engines, the fastest and highest flying planes. Who imagined then that we would be stalled bumper to bumper in gridlock for hours each day as our cars destroy the ozone layer and we inhale the polluting exhaust?

In the United Nations' report on global warming, experts show that the gasses trapped in our atmosphere are heating our planet by several degrees. Among the many disastrous consequences, we are already experiencing drought and skin cancer, floods and extreme weather. And more is coming.

This is the myth of progress. Our children have become the heirs of our errors. In the 1970s the number of children 6 to 11 with asthma surged by 58%. In the 1980s asthma-related deaths increased 23%. Lung-searing, eye-tearing smog destroys lung tissue almost as effectively as chemical weapons.

We are at war with ourselves. We have put our faith in the mythical god of progress and are beginning to see the consequences. Elsewhere in the world, developing nations try to catch up with us. In their desperation they are often even more reckless and destructive. Their people have to flee their lands, which are too depleted and polluted to offer a livelihood. Millions of ecological refugees wander the earth, seeking an environment capable of sustaining their lives.

We must ask, when God promised, in Revelations 21, a new heaven and a new earth, did God have this kind of progress in mind?

The Poor Are Hit the Hardest

Those with the least, always suffer the most. People at the bottom are the first victims of this environmental disaster. While in Appalachia I saw the devastation of that area due to the myth of progress. Factories and mines create new jobs and more income. But the strip mining destroyed the land. The factories dumped dye into the streams. And when the land had been ravaged, the factories moved on, the mines shut down, and the people were left without jobs on useless land.

When visiting the city of McFarland in the lush grape growing valley of Central California, I met many children with cancer. They had played near the fields as low flying airplanes sprayed pesticides on the crops. A mother showed me her child born without arms or legs. No one had warned her of the hazard of working in the fields while she was pregnant. And beyond McFarland's city limits? Those same lethal pesticides are transported to dinner tables everywhere. You can't wash the chemicals out of the grapes.

And who lives closest to our city dumps and toxic waste areas? Usually low income communities and people of color. They have no alternative. And where do we ship our toxic wastes? To poor countries desperate to pay off their national debt. We also send them our labor-intensive industries, because their poor will work for next to nothing.

God gifted humanity with creation for the common good of all, but some of us consume too much. In the United States we use fifty times more energy than people in poor areas of the world. We waste water and destroy topsoil. And where does that leave people without resources and alternatives? Twenty-five thousand people die daily for lack of clean water. Forty thousand children die each day of malnutrition diseases.

As Pope John Paul II said, we must have a new sense of solidarity with all peoples, especially the world's poor. He insists that the industrialized nations cannot deplete the resources of the poorer nations leaving them only waste. We must share creation with one another if we wish to have God's blessings and live in peace. "Today the ecological crisis has assumed such proportions as to be the responsibility of everyone," he wrote.

A New Global Spirituality

Many of us are alarmed, fearful, desperate, even angry. We feel powerless and frustrated. We worry for our children. We sense that our spirituality is inadequate to the challenges of our time. We need a new vision, or is it an old one? It helps to read the stories from Genesis in a way that reflects God's caring and the possibilities of peace.

"In the beginning," the Genesis stories tell us, God made all creation good, and made us partners, caretakers, stewards. "See, I am now establishing my covenant with you and your descendants... and also with every living creature" (Genesis 9:8-10). We share a common destiny, all of us creatures large and small, mighty or humble. Somehow we are all related by God's choice and promise and agreement with us.

Francis understood this covenant. Like Adam who was commissioned to name all creatures, Francis renamed them brothers and sisters. Paul, too, caught the vision. He saw the new creation emerging with us: "All creation awaits with eager expectation the revelation of the children of God... in the hope that creation itself would be set free from slavery to corruption and share in the glorious freedom of the children of God" (Romans 8:19,21).

The Bible has given us some understanding of God's presence in the created world, but nature itself is a book of revelation. As we look through a microscope, we see the incredible complexity and intricacy of all created matter. As we look at the universe, we are awestruck at the magnificence of the stars. Today we know much more of the interconnectedness of all life. To destroy one species is to threaten others. To decimate rain forests on one continent can imperil us all. Nature gives us a new awareness about God's presence and our own interconnectedness.

On a recent hike in the Rockies I encountered a couple with two babies on their backs. I wondered why they would haul tiny children out into the wilderness. They explained that they felt it urgent to give them a sense and appreciation of nature very quickly in life. This early learning may help them live in communion with all creation. That is the way forward. We care for creation, and it cares for us. We respect its beauty and God cares for us all.

The Greening of Religion

Francis longed for harmony with all creation. Today, many people share this vision. We celebrate Earth Day together. We organize for water conservation and form political coalitions to make offenders clean up toxic wastes. We come from many traditions, but we all recognize our oneness with creation.

I have seen bishops, ministers, activists and concerned parents all bow their heads in silent prayer with the spiritual leader of the Western Shoshone Nation at the Nevada Test Site. He prayed for the well-being of all the creatures being desecrated on his tribal land. He was stunned as the bomb exploded beneath us. We all felt the agony of mother earth.

In this crisis of survival, we are seeing the greening of religion. Religious traditions are increasingly sharing a new vocabulary: ecology and creation, responsibility and stewardship, environmental balance and relational interdependence, human rights and nature's rights, and a sacred trust toward the earth. We are experiencing a new global conversion that enables us to participate in creation, and see it as God sees it and loves it. This new creation spirituality and theology is a sign of hope.

To Walk Nonviolently on the Earth

We need a new spirituality for a global awareness and we need a new way of acting in this polluted world. We have to say no to violence, war and environmental destruction. We have to end our exploitation and domination of the earth and the poor. At the same time, we have to say yes to life, solidarity, conservation, dialogue and self-determination. We say yes to creation and all her creatures. From now on, we strive to walk like Francis by treating all creation and all creatures with respect and love, as our sisters and brothers.

We all have needs. We need food, shelter, clothing, medical aid and education. These needs are critical for the seven billion people on earth.

But we have many more wants. We want material possessions and pleasure in abundance. Some define our modern existence this way: "Shop 'till you drop. The one who dies with the most toys wins." These wants can become insatiable. There is an ancient saying: 'To believe you can cure a person's desire for wealth by giving them more money is like thinking you can put out a fire by pouring butterfat on it." It is this craving for more and more and more possessions that is destroying our world.

We are in a struggle for survival. At this moment in history we must choose. If we continue to exploit our planet, it will be destroyed. This means the end of human life, but also of the magnificent creation that has reflected God's presence for billions of years. That is a great tragedy and sin. But it is not too late. If we can come to love creation, to cherish and care for it, we can find solutions.

There are many ways to walk nonviolently on earth. Growing food puts us in touch with God's creative power and also offsets the food shortage. Walking or hiking helps us appreciate nature. Planting trees makes us co-creators with God and also helps absorb the carbon dioxide that is destroying life. Joining the global movement to end the many facets of the growing environmental crisis is a critical practice today. Taking action together we can withdraw our consent from the destruction of the earth and build the constructive foundations for a more sustainable planet for all.

These are both human and religious acts. They register our respect for life. At the same time, this generates happiness. If we walk nonviolently on earth we will discover the joy of Francis as he celebrated life with all brothers and sisters throughout the cosmos.

4

Making Peace Like St. Francis

When Francis lay sick, the bishop of Assisi at the time excommunicated the mayor. In return, the man who was mayor was enraged, and had this proclamation announced, loud and clear, throughout the city of Assisi: no one was to sell or buy anything from the bishop, or to draw up any legal document with him. And so they thoroughly hated each other. Although very ill, Francis was moved to pity for them, especially since there was no one, religious or secular, who was intervening for peace and harmony between them.

— Francis of Assisi: Early Documents, Volume 2

Toward the end of his life, Francis was very sad over the division around him, including ongoing wars. When Assisi went to war with Perugia again, the Pope had tried to stop it by threatening with excommunication anyone who entered into alliances compelling them to go to war with another. But the battle went forward. "Everyone rose up ferociously against his neighbor," one historian writes. The walls oozed fraternal blood. Those inside the city were subjected to hunger, and those outside, to never-ending slaughter... The mayor of Assisi swore on his part to observe the new agreements. It was an open challenge to the pope and the Papal State. Bishop Guido excommunicated the mayor.

The bishop's excommunication of the mayor made him furious. The city was divided and filled with enmity; Francis was deeply upset by this hatred and violence. This was not just a misunderstanding or an argument between the bishop and the mayor. There was serious structural violence involving the nobility, the new merchant class, the city and the Church. In his book *Engaging the Powers: Discernment and Resistance in a World of Domination*, theologian and biblical scholar Walter Wink would

41

name this as an example of the "Domination System" and its efforts to control society. In the case of 13th century Assisi, this struggle turned on the question of who would be in control--the powerful factions of the city or the people allied with the pope?

In Wink's terminology, these institutions are "powers" which enforce domination and preclude peaceful resolution. "What people in the world of the Bible experienced and called 'Principalities and Powers' was in fact real," Wink writes. "They were discerning the actual spirituality at the center of the political, economic and cultural institutions of their day... I use the expression 'the Domination System' to indicate what happens when an entire network of Powers becomes integrated around idolatrous values."

Wink continues: "Any attempt to transform a social system without addressing both its spirituality and its outer forms is doomed to failure." Francis seems to have had an intuitive understanding of this. While fully aware of the demonic nature of the institutions of his times that caused such bloodshed, poverty and suffering, he also addressed the deeper spiritual disease, the thirst for violence, the lack of a sense of reverence for God's creatures, and the failure to appreciate the gift of creation.

Wink writes: "The Powers are good. The Powers are fallen. The Powers must be redeemed." While recognizing the demonic in each of the institutions involved, Francis also acknowledged the source of their creation and sought to restore them to the God-given purpose for which they were created. He did this through example, through intervention and through bestowing God's grace and peace. Francis lived in a world of violence, which sought to bring order over chaos by violence. Into his world of violence Francis introduced the alternative of nonviolence and sought a new culture of peace. Wink sees the Gospel as the alternative power to the Domination System. Francis brought this gospel alternative to new life.

In the particular fight between the mayor and the bishop, Francis was pained to see that no one would intervene to re-establish peace and concord. So he accepted the call of the Gospel to be a "peacemaker."

Francis used his enormous moral capital—the goodwill he held among the people involved—to intervene. Bishop Guido had played a major role in the development of the Franciscan movement, and the mayor was among Francis's most devoted supporters. His daughter Agnes had joined Clare at San Damiano at an early age. Both the bishop and the mayor held Francis in the highest esteem.

Francis used a subtle nonviolent approach. He added another verse on peace to his *Canticle of the Creatures*. He sent one of his brothers to invite the mayor to go to the bishop's palace, and another to prepare the bishop. Francis did not go but remained in prayer. The brothers then sang the canticle with its message of peace to the mayor and the bishop, which included the new verse:

Happy those who endure in peace,
By you, Most High, they will be crowned.

Both were moved to great repentance and a mutual embrace. "In this moment, a centuries-old struggle for power ended," historian Arnoldo Fortini wrote, crediting this intervention with bringing true peace into being.

Walter Wink stresses that a key dimension of nonviolent action is prayer. Wink asserts that prayer and nonviolent action are the means by which we best engage the Powers and achieve victory. Intercession visualizes an alternative future to the one created by the momentum of current forces. We see this exemplified by Francis, who prays in his cell while the brothers engage the opposing powers with the gentleness of Francis's song. Eight centuries after Francis we are called, as he was, to pray and act for a new future of peace.

PART THREE

TO JAIL FOR PEACEMAKING

If anyone wishes to come after me, they must deny themselves take up the cross daily and follow me. Whoever wishes to save their life will lose it, but whoever loses their life for my sake will save it.

— Luke 9: 23-24

We must widen the prison gates and we must enter them as a bridegroom enters the bride's chamber. Freedom is to be wooed only inside prison walls and sometimes on gallows, never in the council chambers, courts, or the schoolroom.

— Mahatma Gandhi

Upholding the Higher Law: Fr. Louie's Life of Nonviolent Action

Although Fr. Louie had a long history of nonviolent action beginning with his work with the United Farm Workers and draft resisters in the 1960s, his first act of nonviolent civil disobedience did not take place until 1980 when he joined a group protesting the University of California's management of the national nuclear weapons laboratories at Los Alamos and Livermore. Later, he shared "how profoundly religious an experience" this overnight sit-in was.

From then on, he frequently participated in spiritually-grounded civil disobedience, including repeated actions at the Nevada Test Site north of Las Vegas, through the Nevada Desert Experience, which he co-founded to end the nuclear testing that had been occurring there since 1951.

Civil disobedience and going to jail for peace have a deeply religious significance for Fr. Louie. "Stepping across the line," he says, "I let go and let God take over." He reports an elation that accompanies this experience and a "sense of being embraced by God." For him, his time in jail echoes the traditional Catholic spiritual retreat, with space and time for prayer and meditation; mindful attentiveness to the rhythm of the day; the opportunity to experience the desolation and listlessness of boredom; and the chance to engage and serve other prisoners.

Jail, for Louie, is not only a kind of religious retreat; it is a reminder of the roots of Christian spirituality: Jesus' incarceration and execution, the jailing and martyrdom of Christians during the first three centuries of the Christian era, and the periodic detention and "disappearance" of Christians and other people of faith and conscience down to the present day. Like Jesus, if one deliberately challenges injustice, one may well face arrest, jail or even death. Louie has even seen his jail experience as a way of reframing and renewing the three vows of Christian religious life: poverty, chastity and obedience.

47

When his thirteen years as a pastor at the inner-city parish of St. Boniface in San Francisco came to an end, Louie began to consider taking part in a nonviolent witness that might mean more than a day or two in jail. He was drawn to join the growing movement to close the School of the Americas at Ft. Benning, Georgia. Those who crossed the line there faced sentences of three to six months in jail.

This section features Louie's letters from four significant jail experiences after civil disobedience actions at Ft. Benning, Georgia and Fort Huachuca, Arizona, which trains US military personnel in torture techniques, in 2002-2003, 2005-2006, 2007-2008 and 2009-2011.

5

Waging Peace From Jail (2002-2003): Guilty...And Inspired!

July 8-12, 2002, Louie Vitale went on trial with 36 other activists for "crossing the line" at the School of the Americas at Ft Benning, Georgia in November 2001. He wrote the following statement during his trial. He was given a sentence of three months, with a delay until October to give him time to finish his pastoral responsibilities at St Boniface Catholic Church in San Francisco, California.

Thirty-seven of us have been on trial here in federal court in Columbus, Georgia. We are on trial for entering Ft. Benning during a demonstration on November 18, 2001 against the School of Americas (SOA), recently renamed as the "Western Hemisphere School for Security Council." The demonstration was in the form of a funeral procession with coffins and crosses. Participants dressed as mourners.

Those on trial have made it clear, in very moving testimonies, what they have experienced in Central and South America. They spoke of the family members of victims who have suffered atrocities, disappearances, and even executions as a result of the actions of graduates of the SOA. The testimonies brought many of us to tears. These testimonies helped us understand how widespread the atrocities have been. Judge-Magistrate Mallon Faircloth has seemed to be interested in our testimonies and allowed us to talk freely and at length. Nevertheless, he readily found us guilty of trespassing.

Before and during the trial, we the defendants and our supporters have had wonderful opportunities to build community. Reference has been made frequently to Martin Luther King's hope for "the beloved community" and we have felt it. I have been very inspired by the commitment of each of the defendants, some as young as 18. Many have shared the cost of facing six months of incarceration for themselves and their families, but it has not deterred their witness. I am also very edified by the large number of supporters who have come to offer their solidarity. It is a great counter-sign to the destructive role of the SOA. We who have been found guilty now await sentencing. We are prepared and ready to face the consequences of our actions because we are very mindful of the victims of the School of the Americas.

6

Waging Peace From Jail (2002-2003): Coming Full Circle: My Return To Nevada

Fr. Louie began serving his three-month prison term at Nellis AFB Federal Prison near Las Vegas, Nevada on October 16, 2002.

Other than a few trips to Las Vegas in my youth to visit the casinos, and a layover at Nellis Air Force Base when I was in the Air Force, my first residence in Las Vegas was in 1968. We Franciscans were invited by Bishop Joseph Green to assess some of the social problems in Las Vegas and offer some remedies. Out of that discernment came a ten-year commitment to a social justice ministry in Southern Nevada.

Local concerns included racial segregation and discrimination, welfare rights issues, housing for the homeless, farm worker exploitation and the plight of immigrants. A community of Franciscans, sisters, and committed lay persons soon developed to address these problems.

We soon became more aware of another issue, the militarization of Nevada, most notably, of the activities of the nearby Nevada Test Site. Our response grew into an international campaign to stop the testing of nuclear weapons. Eventually the Nevada Desert Experience was founded. It brought thousands to the Nevada Test Site for prayer and nonviolent direct action. Lots of folks from many religious groups received their first initiation into the revered tradition of civil disobedience, and jail. Finally, in the 1990s a moratorium on testing was declared.

Long ago, Thomas Merton called the desert "a sacred place," the proverbial Holy Ground of indigenous peoples, hermits,

51

mystics and pilgrims. We have turned the desert of Southern Nevada into the site of nuclear bombs and casinos. The work of the Nevada Desert Experience has been to reclaim the land as Holy Ground and end the evil of preparations for nuclear holocaust.

This land belongs to the Western Shoshone people. It has been illegally appropriated by the U.S. government for evil purposes. It contains the ancient burial grounds of the Shoshone and is their ancestral heritage. Over time, we have developed close ties with the Western Shoshone. We have joined their struggle to reclaim their land. We have learned to love and cherish that land and have been awakened to its sacredness by their spiritual leaders.

In 1979 I was posted in Oakland, California to do administrative service to the Franciscan province. I returned to Las Vegas in 1988 and helped form Pace e Bene Nonviolence Service, a Franciscan based group that promotes nonviolence. We had become convinced that we not only needed to stop nuclear testing, but to also spread the way of nonviolence around the world.

In 1992 I was asked to fill in for three months at Saint Boniface parish in San Francisco. I was subsequently appointed pastor and became involved in a monumental project to retrofit the church, school and friary buildings for earthquake survival and create new ministries in the Tenderloin area of the city. I was happy to be able to continue my involvement in anti-nuclear campaigns along with these local issues, most notably about homelessness and immigration.

During the 1980s, I became involved in the struggle of Central Americans to end their repressive regimes sponsored by the U.S. government. We were all shocked by the of deaths of Archbishop Oscar Romero of San Salvador, the four U.S. churchwomen, the six Jesuits and two female associates, and the thousands of civilians who were killed.

The participation of the United States government in this persecution has been very hard to bear. It was particularly shocking to come to understand the role of the School of the Americas at Fort Benning in Georgia and the major part it has played in training those who carried out these brutal killings. Among other things, the SOA taught the techniques of infiltration, subversion, disappearance, torture and assassination.

Last year I was invited to attend the November assembly of Pax Christi in Georgia, held in conjunction with the annual peace witness at the School of the Americas. I was presented with their "Teacher of Peace" award which I accepted on behalf of the hundreds I have worked with at the Nevada Desert Experience, Pace e Bene, and other peace groups. I was deeply moved by the ten thousand protesters at the annual Sunday event. We processed to the gates of the SOA and recalled the thousands of deaths in Latin America caused by this training center. I joined a small procession that walked around the fence onto the grounds of Fort Benning toward the school itself. We were arrested, prosecuted, tried and now I am on my way back to Las Vegas to serve 90 days in the Federal Prison Camp at Nellis Air Force Base.

I feel I am coming full circle. When I first landed in Las Vegas in 1957 I was part of the military forces. My consciousness at that time was about protecting the freedom of the country and the world.

I joined the Franciscans and emerged in the 60s with a new awareness. I became opposed to war and to the exploitation of poor and marginalized people around the world. Martin Luther King Jr. and Gandhi became my teachers, Cesar Chavez, Dorothy Day and Philip and Daniel Berrigan became my mentors. Many wonderful colleagues emerged along the way. Los Angeles, Las Vegas, the Bay Area were bases for engaging in the struggle for justice and peace.

Visits to Central and South America, Africa, and Asia, became part of my pilgrimage. So have many jails. Somehow returning to Las Vegas, to a federal prison camp at Nellis Air Force Base, seems a special sign. When I called St. James parish in Las Vegas to tell them of my "new assignment" I was told the choir had sung at the camp the previous Sunday. It seemed a good omen. I can hear them singing, "We've come this far by faith, leaning on the Lord, trusting in his Holy Word...He's never failed us yet!" These are dark times. The tragedy of September 11, 2001 haunts us. The fallout has been enormously frightening. The new U.S. policy outlines a global domination that stretches even the boundaries of empire—to the domination of space. We have declared ourselves the sole dominating force in the world. This kind of darkness can only be cast out by prayer, fasting, and nonviolent action. At least I can attempt the first two here at the Nellis Prison Camp.

It will be for me a place to pray, reflect and listen to the Holy Spirit. You accompany me in my heart as I begin this new pilgrimage for peace.

7

Waging Peace From Jail (2002-2003):
Tears and Joy in Prison

Louie wrote this letter while serving his three-month sentence at Nellis Prison Camp. He was released on January 10, 2003.

It has been an amazing twist of fate that I was sent here to Nellis Air Force Federal Prison Camp. We are adjacent to the Nevada Test Site, scene of my many protests over more than two decades. Here at Nellis we are in the midst of a very active Air Force Base where B-52 Stealth and other aircraft practice bombing runs for war in Iraq. Many weapons, including nuclear weapons, are stored here. Being in the midst of such weapons of mass destruction, such violence, calls me deeper to nonviolence. I feel within me a groaning lamentation that cries out over the destruction which such weapons have caused and for that which they now plan.

I am here in prison with 600 men. The "justice system" crushes these poor people, robbing them of the best years of their lives. This also is a terrible violence. At night I look over our dorm and I weep. The other day my cellmate shared his grief over the break-up of his family, and told me, "You can weep in here." So I weep for them and with them. All of this deepens within me a strong resolve to "set prisoners free," to "turn swords into plowshares," to "wage peace," to "feed the hungry and clothe the naked and shelter the homeless."

I am grateful to be part of Pace e Bene, a group committed to moving our world from violence to wholeness. Even as I grieve over our present violent society I have hope, even joy, that a new day of peace will dawn and all those tears will be wiped away. I thank you all for your most encouraging support and assure you of my grateful prayers. Pace e Bene!

8

Returning To Prison (2005-2006):
A New Monastery – Muscogee County Jail

*In November 2005, Louie again engaged in civil disobedience at Fort
Benning at the annual School of the Americas Watch protest. After his
arrest he was sentenced to six months in prison.*

Franciscan Father Jerry Zawada and I are spending six months in
the Muscogee County Jail. Our new "Monastery" adds a new
vow of "stability" to our vows of poverty, charity and obedience.
With the blessings of our provincial ministers, we traveled to Fort
Benning, in Columbus, Georgia, for the annual commemoration
of the martyrs of Central America. Some 19,000 people gathered
as we marked the anniversary of the Jesuit martyrs of San
Salvador. We also recalled the four North American
churchwomen, Archbishop Romero, the people of El Mozote, and
the thousands of other victims.

The Sunday procession began with thousands of marchers
bearing crosses and others carrying black coffins. Someone
chanted the names of the dead with the entire crowd responding
"Presente!" Jerry and I were privileged to carry one of the coffins.

We marched to an opening in the fence where we slipped
under the first of three fences erected to keep protesters off the
premises. As we knelt in prayer on the other side of the fence,
military officials approached us and took us into custody. Later,
on the bus, I engaged in conversation with a military police
officer. I asked him which leader he would follow if he were
called to kill in battle—Jesus or his military superior. "I shouldn't
be having this conversation with you," he said, ending our talk.

Now we are living in the "Old Men's" cell reserved for
inmates fifty years or older. We hear stories of loss — of

separation from parents, brothers and sisters, spouses and children
— and we hear of the desperate efforts to hang on to their family
ties. We hear stories of their attempts to win freedom in the
courts, to try again, or to deal with their situation. I am reminded
of the plea in Isaiah 61, read by Jesus in the Nazareth Synagogue
(Luke 4) to "Give release to the captives and set the prisoners
free." I would gladly open the door, release the prisoners, and shift
the funds used to maintain this and many other prisons to restore
their families and communities.

These days we remember the 25th anniversary of the
martyrdom of the four churchwomen killed on December 2, 1980,
in El Salvador by graduates of the School of the Americas. And
we are prayerfully mindful of the four Christian Peacemaker
Team members captured in Iraq. We ask ourselves: Is there is no
end to the violence, torture and war making? We share these
concerns with our cellmates and they pray with us, grieve with us.
Our nightly Bible study reminds us of God's accompaniment
through all of this. Someone sent us this quotation from Dietrich
Bonhoeffer, published after his death in *Letters and Papers from
Prison*: "There remains an experience of incomparable value...to
see the great evils of world history from below, from the
perspective of the outcast, the maltreated, the powerless, the
oppressed, the reviled—in short from the perspective of those who
suffer, to look with new eyes on all matters great and small." Yes,
we are learning from our brothers and sisters, and they from us.
They teach us about survival and weakness. We see their intrinsic
goodness, even in the face of crushing structural violence. We all
grow in hope.

The other day, we even had an opportunity to witness to
nonviolence. When I mentioned that some of my envelopes were
missing, the entire cell grew indignant and insisted that the "thief"
be discovered or be forced out by whatever means necessary.
When we pointed out the contradiction with the passages we were
studying regarding Jesus, mercy and his eagerness to forgive, an

amazing transformation took place. The unity of our little community was restored and members professed new awareness of mercy and nonviolence.

We do learn from each other. It is good to be here.

As a postscript to Louie's prison experiences from this period, here is a reflection he wrote after his second long prison stint about being a peacebuilder behind bars:

Having mainly gone to prison for efforts related to peace, it seemed logical to focus on peacebuilding. This was not an easy thing to do. Any kind of organizing in prison is disallowed. But opportunities do arise.

Most recently I spent two six month terms for witnessing at Ft. Benning, Georgia's School of the Americas. I started my sentences in the County detention center. In the Quad I was in (housing about 50) we were in clusters of several double bunks. In our cluster we began a Bible sharing group. It was well attended and quite animated.

One day I noticed that I seemed to be missing some stamps. I was afraid they may have dropped down to the lower bunk and were kept there. I mentioned this to one of the leaders of the Bible study group whose bunk was across from mine. I did not want to make an issue of it, but he immediately took it to the unit.

He called out that someone had stamps stolen, and if the person did not admit to it and ask for a move to another unit, he would be "hurt" and forced out (implying he knew who). I was very upset. I was not even sure if I had used them, given them to another or just misplaced them.

I did not want any violence. I finally went to the leader reminding him that we had just been discussing "Love your enemies," "Judge not and you shall not be judged," words of Jesus from the Bible. He responded that this is prison and we have a code, anyone stealing must be punished and leave the unit, even if it was not certain they had the right culprit. I was very apprehensive and waiting for the attack to happen, probably right at my bunk.

But the leader came to me and said, this was very hard to do, but he had been thinking and praying about the words of Jesus and agreed it was the right thing to do.

As long as I was there the group continued to reflect on this incident and the teachings of Jesus the Peacemaker and there was peace!

9

Behind Prison Walls Again (2007-2008)
November 7, 2007

In September 2007, Louie and Fr. Steve Kelly were arrested at Fort Huachuca, Arizona, headquarters of the U.S. Army Intelligence and the place of trainings for military "interrogators" at Guantanamo Bay and Abu Ghraib. U.S. military personnel are taught how to torture. On October 17, 2007 both priests were sentenced to five months in federal prison, which they began serving immediately. Louie wrote the following letters during this prison experience.

Dear Friends,

So I am back in prison again. We were arrested for trespassing while attempting to take a letter to Gen. Barbara Fast to speak to her and the trainees about the trainings that are happening there, especially regarding "enhanced interrogation." Thus began a yearlong saga, with eight court appearances in Federal Court in Tucson resulting in five month sentences for trespassing and not obeying an officer.

So here I am a federal prisoner, housed in the Imperial County Jail in El Centro, California. We began together in Florence, Arizona. We were separated abruptly on Halloween night; Steve remains there. Who knows why. I am told I will do my remaining time here.

This is a reflective time for me. I have learned a lot more about torture, especially from the great presentation our lawyer, Bill Quigley, made for us from the many reports done by General Taguba in Abu Ghraib in Iraq and other horrific prisons and foreign renditions. This built upon my experiences last year in Jordan and Syria, meeting actual survivors of Abu Ghraib, as well as torture survivors gathered by

Sr. Dianna Ortiz in Washington D.C. last fall. I find myself crying in the night as I draw them into my consciousness.

Last week Carlos Mauricio, a torture survivor from El Salvador who won a landmark conviction and multi-million dollar judgment against Salvadoran generals in a Florida court, and torture victims showed up at a late visiting hour. They are on a caravan travelling to the Ft. Benning protest on November 18th. The cycle goes on.

Last year we were shocked to hear of U.S. torture policies in defiance of the Geneva Conventions. We felt exonerated in our protests by the transition of U.S. Attorneys General. We were notified that a major challenge to a new Attorney General was torture policy (e.g. "Waterboarding"). While aghast at the outcome, we are hopeful that there is a new vigilance in the land.

Meanwhile 20,000+ will gather at Ft. Benning next week and many at Ft. Huachuca and we will say louder and louder: "Not in our name – we will not torture any of God's creatures – never more." We are most grateful for your awesome support!

"Yours in chains,"
Louie

10

Behind Prison Walls Again (2007-2008):
November 11, 2007

As I sit in a solitary cell as a federal prisoner, I reflect on the very recent act of beatification of Franz Jaggerstatter of Austria by Pope Benedict XVI. Franz refused to fight for the Nazis and was beheaded on August 9, 1943.

On October 26, 2007 he received the infallible approval of the church that canonized those early martyrs. Just before he died, Franz dreamt that the leaders of his nation were on "a train to Hell." Franz jumped off – and won the crown of heaven.

As I reflect in my stark cell – which I have "consecrated" in his name—I pray before the Holy card of Blessed Franz sent to me from the beatification ceremony by John Dear. This holy card rests on the metal mirror on the cell's bare wall together with a card from the Carmel of Reno and many of the great women and men peacemakers of our time. As I pray I ask to be included in their midst and for all of us to have the strength to jump off of the train of horrendous violence of our times. This may sound boastful, but it is the boast of Paul and Jesus. It is a mandate to bear Christ the peacemaker to our world.

As I pray here in the early hours—we are awakened at 2:30 A.M. for breakfast—I feel the deep unity in the heart of Christ of which Franz spoke and draw in all those imprisoned here (mostly Mexican nationals) and dare to unite all torture survivors who share such cells in a far more monstrous way. Today we vow to get off that most lucrative, opulent, highly armed – with world destroying nuclear weapons – train to Hell before we blow not just the train but all creation "to Hell."

John Dear sent a reflection—"The Beatification of Franz Jaggerstatter"—which is consoling, inspiring and uplifting. Let the words of Blessed Franz guide our thoughts and actions in the way of peace:

> "We need no rifles or pistols for our battles but instead spiritual weapons...Let us love our enemies, bless those who curse us, pray for those who persecute us. For love will conquer and will endure for all eternity. And happy are they who live and die in God's love."
>
> "If one harbors no thought of vengeance against others and can forgive everyone, [they] will be at peace in [their] heart—and what is more lovely than peace? Let us pray to God that a real and lasting peace may soon descend upon this world."
>
> "The commandments of God teach us, of course, that we must render obedience to secular rulers but only to the extent that they do not order us to do anything evil for we must obey God rather than [human beings]."
>
> "There have always been heroes and martyrs who gave their lives for their faith. If we hope to reach our goal some day that we too must become heroes of the faith."

Blessed Franz, pray for us — give us your vision, wisdom and courage. Make us truly "instruments of peace."

Peace and all good,
Louie

11

Behind Prison Walls Again (2007-2008):
December 2007

Each year a growing number gather at Fort Benning, GA to memorialize the 'martyrs' that have been massacred at the hands of very repressive regimes in Latin America. As we looked at the massacres we were aware of the "enhanced" cruel and excruciating torture that accompanied these deaths. As we focused on the School of the Americas, which trained many of Latin America's military officers, we discovered there were manuals issued in Spanish used at the school to teach methods of torture. These manuals were prepared at the U.S. Army intelligence school at Fort Huachuca in Southern Arizona.

As the scandal of torture spread not just to our Latin American trainees but our own soldiers at Abu Ghraib in Iraq and Guantanamo Bay in Cuba, we became aware that our overzealous desire to engage in the "War on Terror" was stirring our own military and intelligence forces to use the same tactics used elsewhere in what has become known as "enhanced interrogation." The parameters of these are spelled out in a series of memos whose approval evolves from the highest government echelons (even accredited to presidential wartime powers). These circumvent even the Geneva Conventions, a treaty the U.S. co-signed. They also violate our own codes of treatment for enemies and prisoners of war.

Steve Kelly, S.J. and I became aware in October, 2006 that a growing number of people, inspired by participation with School of the Americas Watch, were now gathering at Fort Huachuca to raise attention to the development and transmission of these cruel "enhancements" of interrogation. We became aware that the new commander of Fort Huachuca, General Barbara Fast, had been in command of the interrogations at Abu Ghraib and of the atrocities now so familiar. So on November 19, 2006, we went to visit Gen. Fast.

We were not allowed to deliver our letters to Gen. Fast. We attempted to negotiate a means of delivery and in desperation, we knelt and prayed. We were arrested that day charged with Federal trespass, and released. Then years of court appearances in Tucson, Arizona followed.

Our exceptional lawyer, Bill Quigley, offered to the court several highly reputable, and graphic studies, such as the one prepared by General Taguba for the U.S. Army, one by the U.S. Red Cross, one by the American Civil Liberties Union, and others. At the government's request, Judge Hector Estrada did not allow any of this information to be used during these proceedings.

Steve and I did not engage in this pursuit to avoid the possible penalties stemming from our actions. We felt an urgent mandate on behalf of the human community to raise the visibility of this inhumane behavior being carried out in our name, causing such suffering to so many, and creating untold scandal to the world community. General Taguba revealed to us that he did not release the worst of the pictures, as he did not believe people could take it. He did tell us "history would honor our actions." We could not bring this testimony to a jury, but it did get an airing. One year later we are gratified by these efforts.

Steve and I are serving our time. Three hundred people gathered at Fort Huachuca on November 18 to offer their support. Yes – we must agree torture is always evil and is being put on trial in the U.S. And we are saying "No, never again. Not in our name!"

12

Behind Prison Walls Again (2007-2008)
March 2008

Dear Friends:

Many, many thanks for your support during our nonviolent civil disobedience at Ft. Huachuca, Arizona, during the action, the long trial process, and this time of our incarceration. We started our imprisonment at the federal contract facility in Florence, AZ. After two weeks I was suddenly called to "roll it up" at about 11p.m. on Halloween night. We gave a few treats to our cellmates, but got the trick ourselves. Steve held out a few more weeks until he was moved to a federal facility in Taft, California.

I had learned at Columbus, Georgia, that some jails and prisons have a "senior section." As my sister told me, at 76 we need all the help we can get. These sections are quieter. Medical services are more readily available. Announcements are loud and clear. Some of us get lower bunks, etc.

The section is technically a "minimum segregated housing unit" (S.H.U.) where you might be alone in the cell except for an hour out in the day. If there are no other restrictions on your presence you may have a cellmate and could be in a small group that goes into the day room (which also houses the showers, phone, television, etc.) or on the occasional trip to the yard for exercise (maybe once a week for about an hour).

Since I am a "senior fellow," I am neither a target nor an aggressor. Most of the time I have had a cellmate, usually for a week or two at a time, and then they move off to court, camp, or another federal facility. Presently, we are a group of five or six. As the elder member, I am "Don Vitale." The sergeant in charge appreciates the "calm" and hints at keeping me longer. He said he might put me on the payroll.

So I am an old guy who lives in a S.H.U. like the nursery rhyme: "There was an old woman who lived in a shoe. She had so many children, she didn't know what to do!"

The latter phrase describes the place; the old man describes the circumstances. So I am in one of the small two-person cells, sometimes alone, sometimes with another (usually a young Mexican man) and usually part of a group for an hour or a day.

No, this old man "who lives in a SHU" doesn't have children, but I do think of these young guys as *"mi hijos."* The rest of the verse – "not knowing what to do with them" — is seeing the desperation of their lives. Two of them have attempted suicide. Some face near life-long sentences for drugs.

I'm sure the older lady who lived in a shoe in the nursery rhyme nevertheless felt blessed by her children, loved and cared for them, and welcomed with joy their presence and affection.

So yes, I welcome each one that enters my cell or group and try to help them in any way I am able.

We had a really nice Ash Wednesday "liturgy." We have some other prayers, liturgy, and bible studies (mostly in the cell), which are always well received.

Martin Sheen visited recently. They brought him through the jail and into our cell and that gave us a bit of notoriety. Most of the group is very supportive of our actions, and most of the staff seems sympathetic.

I am very grateful to be here. It is a privilege to be able to share at least in a small way in the oppression and suffering of those in prison.

May all of us increase our efforts to eliminate torture.

With Much Gratitude,
Louie

13

Behind Prison Walls Again (2007-2008)
March 2008: Letter from Imperial County Jail

It was the evening of October 16, 2007. Fr. Stephen Kelly, S.J. and I were due in court the next day for our nonviolent witness against torture nearly a year earlier. That night we received a call from Major General Antonio Taguba, the man who wrote the Pentagon's report on the Abu Ghraib prison scandal in Iraq. He told us, "History will honor your actions." The next day a magistrate in a Tucson, Arizona courtroom reached a different conclusion, and sent us to prison for five months.

And so I write from the Imperial County Jail in El Centro, California, behind bars for challenging the training of interrogators at the U.S. Army Intelligence Center and School based at Ft. Huachuca, Arizona. In November 2006, Fr. Kelly and I had gone to Ft. Huachuca to deliver a letter opposing the teaching of torture. We hoped to speak with enlisted personnel about the illegality and immorality of torture, but were arrested as we knelt in prayer halfway up the driveway at the Army base.

Mohandas Gandhi said that the cell door is the door to freedom. In freely entering the Imperial prison in India – and, here, the Imperial County Jail in California -- there is nothing more to fear. It is here that we achieve a transformation, a turning, a *teshvua*, the Hebrew term for "repentance." Here we discover the path of resistance: a vocation that we must follow in the midst of empire to overcome the oppression of our brothers and sisters.

I realize this stance in my solitary cell. As the steel doors clang shut, there is a freedom to surrender to God and the universe. There is a freedom to be open to the creative call of compassion towards the global community.

For me it begins here with those in this prison who have been cast aside by our society. Those who have been rejected, I see as brothers and sisters, attempting to live good lives in the face of severe social, economic and personal obstacles.

I have come to this prison cell because I was moved to challenge a terrible frontier that my country has crossed into in its ill-conceived and ill-fated war in Iraq: torture.

Each of us has had to absorb the reality that ours is a nation that tortures. By its policies and practices, the United States has retracted the binding commitment it made when it signed the 1975 *Declaration Against Torture*. Adopted by the U.N. General Assembly, the declaration prohibited torture, which it defined in Article 1 as: "Any act by which severe pain or suffering, whether physical or mental, is intentionally inflicted by or at the instigation of a public official on a person for such purposes as obtaining from him or a third person information or confession, punishing him for an act he has committed, or intimidating him or other persons."

As shocking as watching the World Trade Towers collapse on September 11, 2001 was seeing, in 2004, the startling pictures of raw torture perpetrated by the U.S. military at Abu Ghraib prison in Iraq.

General Taguba reported at a conference held at the University of San Francisco that the torture photos were only the tip of the iceberg. He feared for the sensitivities of the viewers if he released the bulk of the incriminating photos.

We have since become aware of the extent of these so-called enhanced interrogation methods—hangings, electric shock, beatings, waterboarding and other extreme physical and psychological procedures—spelled out in memos emanating from the White House. They have been used in other prisons in Iraq, Guantanamo Bay, Cuba, and in renditions to other countries such as Syria. We outsource our enemy combatant captives for torture so that we can disclaim any responsibility.

While in Jordan and Syria in the summer of 2006, I spoke with Iraqis who had been imprisoned by the U.S. in Abu Ghraib. (They

69

were dumbfounded to hear that some of us had gone to prison to protest their imprisonment and treatment.) Meeting them convinced me that what this policy and practice of torture represents has diminished our standing in the worldwide community.

Many say torture is worse than killing in war. It destroys not only the body but also the spirit. This is true not only for the victims, but also for the torturer. By extension, this is surely true for the countries involved. Major religious bodies attest that torture is immoral, sinful, evil, and always wrong.

Alyssa Peterson, a young U.S. Army interpreter, went through training with interrogators of the U.S. Army Intelligence School at Ft. Huachuca. She was sent as part of an interrogation team to one of the U.S. prisons in Iraq. After just two sessions in the cages, she objected, and refused to participate in the harsh interrogation techniques. She became distraught and was sent to suicide prevention training, only to commit suicide shortly thereafter. ("U.S. Soldier Killed Herself After Objecting to Interrogation Techniques," Greg Mitchell, November 01, 2006, *Editor & Publisher*.)

This story stunned Steve Kelly and me. It prompted us to join a protest at Ft. Huachuca focusing on interrogator training.

The commander at Ft. Huachuca, Major General Barbara Fast, had been chief of military intelligence in Iraq. She was stationed at Abu Ghraib during the height of the abuses, yet has never been reprimanded nor prosecuted for her command failure to prevent it. We wanted to ask her about the training of interrogators, because we understood that in the summer of 2002, Brig. Gen. John Custer, then second in command of Ft. Huachuca (and who in 2007 succeeded General Fast as Commander), went to Guantanamo on special assignment. Upon his return, he integrated the techniques he learned about at Guantanamo into standard practices. ("New Intel Course Trains Al Qaeda interrogation," *Army News Service*, Feb. 24, 2003.) Fort Huachuca is already notorious as the source of the torture manuals used at the School of the Americas — we wondered what other secrets were still untold?

So we brought a letter requesting a meeting with General Fast, the trainers, and the trainees, but were stopped before reaching the gate. We knelt, we prayed and we were arrested. Now we are serving five-month sentences as federal prisoners.

Three more activists were arrested engaging in nonviolent civil disobedience at the base on November 18, 2007, and were sentenced to supervised probation and a $5,000 fine or 500 hours of community service. Two of the three spent two months in jail without bail while awaiting trial.

As a nation, we have crossed a line that we had pledged we would never cross.

Jesus boldly challenged every barrier to justice, fearlessly breaking the innumerable taboos, customs, and laws that dehumanize, destroy, or diminish human beings. His life and vision pushes me to say "no" to injustice and "yes" to love in action. As a Catholic Franciscan, I have in turn been deeply influenced by the vision and spirituality of Francis of Assisi who brought Jesus' vision alive in concrete and powerful ways in his own time. In the thirteenth century, Francis had an enormous impact on society. Caught up at first in the merchant economy of his father and the grandeur of war, he became a participant and victim of war. After a year as a prisoner of war, he came to see the evil of war and violence.

Though he had originally been attracted to the valor and heroism of the Crusades, he realized that we could only approach our fellow creatures with gestures of openness and love. He rejected the Crusader's violence and passed through their lines to embrace the Sultan. Francis challenged the brothers who followed him to live among Muslims and be subject to them in order to learn their truth. We must follow these insights if we wish to realize peace.

The cell door clangs shut. I am alone. Instead of trying to escape this solitude, I enter it deeply: *This is where I am.* Here in this

71

empty cell I have begun to experience prison in the way James W. Douglass in *Resistance and Contemplation* describes it: not as "an interlude in a white middle class existence, but as a stage of the Way redefining the nature of my life." I have sensed this transformation, little by little. These days are a journey into a new freedom and a slow transformation of being and identity: an invitation to enter my truest self, and to follow the road of prayer and nonviolent witness wherever it will lead.

I am in this little hermitage in the presence of God, in the presence of the Christ who gave his life for the healing and well-being of all. I am also in the presence of the vast cloud of witnesses, some of whom are represented in the icons that have multiplied in this cell, gifts sent to me from people everywhere: Oscar Romero, Martin Luther King, Jr., Dorothy Day, Steven Biko, the martyrs of El Salvador, John XXIII. All those who have given their lives to fashion a more human world. At the same time, I experience a deep connection with my fellow prisoners and with those outside these prison walls, including those who have sent me many letters and expressions of prayer and support.

In my empty cell, I experience a growing awareness of the communion of saints — and of the possibility of a world where the vast chasm of violence and injustice enforced by torture and war is bridged and transformed. Here, I feel a new sense of hope, and await the coming of the Kingdom of God.

Fr. Louie was released from prison on March 14, 2008. Five days later, he participated in a "die-in" with hundreds of people in a busy street in downtown San Francisco, California to mark the fifth anniversary of the war in Iraq

.

14

Birthdays for a Prisoner (2010-2011)
Summer 2010

Fr. Louie served a six-month federal prison sentence beginning in early 2010 imposed after engaging in nonviolent action at Ft. Benning, Georgia in November 2009 in which he called for the closure of the School of the Americas by prayerfully walking onto the base. He received numerous letters marking his 78th birthday on June 1st. Given the volume of mail, Louie asked Pace e Bene to send the following letter of his to all birthday well wishers.

Thank you so much for your recent note and its birthday greeting! I appreciate your helping me celebrate my 78th birthday – and I am so grateful for your support!

One of the highlights of the day in prison is "Mail Call." It often is announced with a loud call, and draws people together within hearing range and near enough to receive an envelope.

One of the delights of being a "Prisoner of Conscience" is that there is strong group support. Fortunately, with groups such as the School of the Americas Watch and Pace e Bene, there are enough messages of support that the gratifying feeling of having done the right thing more than balances the sense of deprivation felt in prison. My mail averages about 15 pieces a day. In addition, I receive a mailing with several print-outs from "Common Dreams," sent by a lawyer friend of mine.

Answering the many pieces of mail is a challenge, but it is one I enjoy very much. Sometimes I do feel desperate that I cannot keep up. I hope you all understand the delays; there are many restrictions on outgoing mail with special labels with significant limitations on the number I'm allowed each day, restrictions on only 20 stamps per week, etc. I wish I could reply sooner to each of you.

I am deeply grateful to all of you who have eased the sense of deprivation and given me the needed support for the duration. You fill my time and my spirit with hope and joy, and most profoundly a deep sense of being loved and cared for. I think this sentiment has been communicated to my inmate companions and even the custodial officers. I thank you from the bottom of my heart, and give thanks to God for all the letters, a few visits (regrettably hard to arrange, especially with a short sentence here), prayers, and your good thoughts.

Thank you also for your continued efforts to bring attention to the plight of victims of torture and war, for efforts to bring about the closing of the SOA (WHINSEC), and also for your support of Pace e Bene and our pursuit of a world of peace and nonviolence.

I look forward to seeing many of you on the "outside" with an opportunity to express my deep gratitude in person and share a few stories (yes, we share many laughs here as well).

Peace and all goodness!
Louie

Louie was released from prison in July 2010, but crossed the line once again at the School of the Americas in November of that year. He was immediately sentenced and began serving six more months in prison. Upon his release in May of 2011 Pace e Bene celebrated his 79th birthday at the National Shrine of St. Francis in San Francisco, CA.

Welcomed by former county supervisor Angela Alioto, Louie's community came together to share their heartfelt love and support for him and to affirm the importance of the kind of nonviolent resistance Louie's actions at Ft. Benning represented.

The event began in the late afternoon with Louie celebrating mass in a replica of a tiny chapel that Saint Francis of Assisi renovated at the beginning of his spiritual journey. The birthday party that followed *included music by singer-songwriter Francisco Herrera and by the St. Boniface Gospel Choir, from the church that Louie pastored for thirteen years.*

The event was highlighted by an opening ritual by Veronica Pelicaric and a series of moving toasts by Daniel Ellsberg, Sr. Mary Litell, Laura Slattery, Dolores Priem, Friar Josef, and Louie's sister, Marie Fielding. Anne Symens-Bucher belted out "Hello Louie!" to the tune of "Hello Dolly!" Then Louie was interviewed in a "fireside chat" by Ken Butigan.

Just before birthday cake was shared by all, activist and author Fr. John Dear led the community in a blessing of Louie as he prepared for the next phase of his peacemaking journey.

Louie Vitale at St. Catherine's
Military Academy

Louie Vitale baptizing his nephew

Louie Vitale Meeting Pope John Paul II

A young Friar Louie Vitale

Louie preparing to cross the line at the School of the Americas in 2009

Louie Vitale with other co-founders of Pace e Bene

Louie praying at Livermore Labs

Louie Vitale receiving an Honorary Doctorate at CTU

Louie Vitale with Dolores Huerta and Sherri Maurin

Louie with Pace e Bene staff, volunteers and associates in 2011

Louie at his 79th birthday party after his release from a six month prison sentence.

Louie with Dan Ellsberg

Louie joining an interfaith candlelight vigil during Occupy Oakland

Louie with friend and fellow Franciscan Jerry Zawada

Louie celebrating mass at his 79th birthday party

Louie joining hands in prayer at Vandenberg Air Force Base

Louie praying at the Nagasaki Peace Memorial in Japan

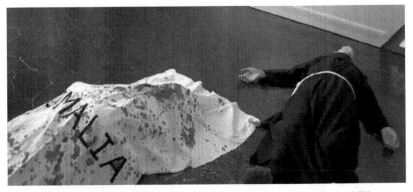

Louie staging a "die-in" at the Mandalay Bay Casino in Las Vegas, NV
during a drone convention in 2012

Louie participating in the NDE
Sacred Peace Walk 2012

Louie at the Nevada Test Site during
the CNV Week of Actions 2014

Louie at San Francisco BART Station
singing for peace during CNV Week of
Actions 2015

Louie with friends at the Campaign
Nonviolence National Conference 2015

PART FOUR

FROM WAR AND INJUSTICE TO THE WAY OF NONVIOLENCE

Nonviolence is the greatest force at the disposal of mankind. It is mightier than the mightiest weapon of destruction.

— Mohandas Gandhi

'No' to war and violence and 'Yes' to dialogue and peace! With war, one always loses. The only way to win a war is never to wage it… Ban nuclear weapons and all weapons of mass destruction.

— Pope Francis, August 9, 2015, 70th anniversary of U.S. atomic bombing of Nagasaki

War is the negation of all rights and a dramatic assault on the environment. If we want true integral human development for all, we must work tirelessly to avoid war between nations and between peoples.

— Pope Francis, Address to the United Nations, September 25, 2015

Woundedness and Sacredness: Fr. Louie's Reflections on Violence and Nonviolence in Our Times

In 1989, Fr. Louie Vitale, Sr. Rosemary Lynch, OSF, Peter Ediger and Julia Occhiogrosso founded Pace e Bene Nonviolence Service to support the emergence of a more just, peaceful and sustainable world through active nonviolence. It organized trainings, workshops, seminars. It took nonviolent action with a growing number of campaigns and movements. It created resources for change, including a series of books and monographs.

It also published a quarterly newsletter entitled The Wolf of Pace e Bene, whose title derived from the story of Saint Francis's peacemaking between a fierce wolf and the town of Gubbio. In addition to news about Pace e Bene's trainings, actions, and resources, this publication typically included one or two longer reflections on the issues of the day in light of nonviolence. The following section is comprised of a series of these pieces Louie wrote over the years.

In re-reading these essays two decades on, one is sharply aware of the seismic changes since then. The Cold War had just ended, and there was a hope that this would set the world on a fundamentally new course, with old enmities giving way to cooperation and military spending redirected to meet human needs. Instead, the geopolitical lines dramatically shifted, with the Persian Gulf War, the sanctions imposed on Iraq, and the fracturing of the Oslo peace process in Israel/Palestine. The attacks on the U.S. on September 11, 2001— and the subsequent U.S. war on terror, passage of the Patriot Act, and invasions and occupations of Afghanistan and Iraq—accelerated a global tsunami, as did the Great Recession of 2008.

At the same time, multiple waves of nonviolent resistance and transformation have also washed over our world, beginning with people power movements that thwarted a coup in the former USSR and ended oppressive regimes throughout Latin America, South

Africa, Indonesia, East Timor, Serbia, Georgia, Liberia and the Arab Spring in Tunisia and Egypt.

All of these developments would be in the future when most of the following essays were penned. They focus on matters that Friar Louie was deeply concerned about—the World War II generation and how it had impacted the world; the beating of Rodney King in 1992; the woundedness of Las Vegas, where Louie lived throughout the 1990s; and the importance of establishing a just immigration policy.

In each of these chapters, Louie brings both his Franciscan vision of peace and justice and his own social location—living among those who have most often been ignored and despised, but also his own choice to take nonviolent action in movements seeking to heal and transform a culture that systematically ignores and despises those at the margins.

15

Exposing The Myth

Fall 1999. Louie recalls being raised into a culture of American patriotism where violence and war is the ultimate sacrifice and honor. Yet he later recognizes the myth found within that long-told story.

I was born at the height of The Great Depression. This was seen as a low point in our national history. As we recovered from this severe economic malaise, war clouds descended on the horizon. As a child I had some awareness of the impending war with Adolph Hitler. My father gathered us as a family together to explain that even though we came from Italy, we were Americans and we would be on the side of the Allies in a war against Germany and Italy.

As a boy of nine years old, I can still remember President Franklin Roosevelt announcing that the Japanese had bombed Pearl Harbor and that we were at war. There are many war memories for those of us growing up during that era. My father took me to newsreels in which we saw graphic scenes of our boys in combat, and our victories. We also had relatives and friends in the war and saw blue stars and even gold stars in their mothers' windows. We had to endure gas rationing and engage in air raid drills. I went with my Dad to the San Francisco Bay Area to help him move my grandmother, still an Italian citizen, away from the coast lest she signal Italian submarines from the Berkeley shore.

All of this, nevertheless, was part of the war effort, and we were patriotic. I had many war toys and fought my own battles. I watched with glee every Allied victory. We went downtown in Los Angeles for the V-E Day Celebration watching the ticker tape from the office windows and the sailors grabbing the girls and kissing them on Main Street. I was filled with pride when I heard that we had dropped the atom bomb in Japan. And then the war was over. We had an unconditional surrender. We had won!

No one in my world questioned any of this. I visited with a friend of my Uncle's who was a judge who tried conscientious objectors. Surely they were un-American. We watched many war films. They were formative for my coming to manhood. Only much later did I learn that 1600 films of the 2500 produced in those years were financed by the War Department.

I was formed by the dominant myth of our era. A myth is the overarching story we tell ourselves as individuals and as whole cultures. The myth that ruled during World War II told us that the world was in terrible danger. We were destined by God to save it. We rose to the challenge. We engaged in a massive build-up of the war industry. Our country was able to supply the mightiest land, sea and air force in the history of the world. We came to the rescue of the free world and we won.

It is my contention that the men of my era operated out of this myth. Furthermore, this myth was so deeply planted that it encouraged the people of the United States to spend trillions of dollars after the war to remain the mightiest land, sea and air force in history. Even when a cold war with Russia escalated from the first atomic bombs into a nuclear arms race, it bankrupted the world's economies and recklessly threatened (and still does) the survival of the earth itself.

My part in living out this myth was to spend a few years in the U. S. Air Force following graduation from R.O.T.C. at Loyola University in Los Angeles. As I reflect on those years it makes me conscious of how much I had bought into this view of the world. Although I was reluctant to be part of a bomber crew and actually drop nuclear weapons on cities, I was ready to shoot down the Russian bombers to defend our people. I was not even thwarted after having been sent to shoot down a positively identified Russian bomber only to find out it was an airliner. It even occurred to me that I should make this a career; after all, our fighters were now being outfitted with nuclear missiles.

Fortunately, by the grace of God I was led to the Franciscans where my consciousness began to shift. Through many years of exposure to the Gospel, to some wonderful socially active friars, and the example of Martin Luther King, Jr. and Cesar Chavez, with whom the Franciscans had a close association, I began to see through the myth. We were not protecting the free world, but using it for our own interests. Even the least militant U.S. president, Jimmy Carter, signed Presidential Directive 54 that we would go to war—yes, even nuclear war—to protect our interests in the Persian Gulf. Both Bush presidencies eventually led us to war in that part of the world.

The myth of our maintaining the world's peace through the mightiest land, sea and air forces is unraveling. We have not been able to keep the world free from war—quite the opposite. The resources wasted are astounding. But even more shocking is that it is all unnecessary and counterproductive. The myth stands exposed. Although this has become apparent as we look at the fallout from this military policy, it is even more revealing as we look at what is really transforming the world. What is really leading us toward a world of peace is not "the mightiest land, sea and air force" but "people power."

Walter Wink has documented how the wave of nonviolence that brought dramatic transitions throughout the world sweeping through the Philippines, South Africa, most of Eastern Europe and notably the Soviet Union resulted in a nonviolent transformation that affected almost two-thirds of all the peoples of the world.

Yet when I speak publicly of nonviolence I find that this myth is still alive and well. "But what if.... ?"

We learn slowly.

But the evidence is in. Freedom has come not through military power but through nonviolent people power.

Nonviolence works. This must be our new myth, our new story.

We are grateful to the pioneers of nonviolence who are showing us the way: Jesus, the prophets, St. Francis, Gandhi, Martin Luther King, Jr., Dorothy Day, Cesar Chavez, the Berrigans and many others. Though sometimes ridiculed, these advocates of nonviolence have been proven to be right. Indeed, they are essential to the salvation of humankind and our planet.

16

The Consequences Of World War II

1994. Louie remembers the cost of World War II and imagines the path of nonviolence that could be pursued in the future.

On the fiftieth anniversary of D-Day, the spectacular battle in Normandy, France that led to the end of Second World War in Europe, Newsweek summed up the impact of the war in this way: "World War II simultaneously saved democracy and changed the way we live. What could be more relevant to the second half of the 20th century than that?"

I do not have any doubt that World War II dramatically affected the second half of the 20th century and, now, the 21st. My purpose here is not to write a critique of the war but to reflect on its legacy. Did it really save democracy and save the world?

Since 1945, we have lived under threat in unprecedented ways. Our relations with much of the world have been under the threat of nuclear extinction. We have seen the enormous ecological destructiveness of the atomic age. Nuclear weapons have been threatened in many international skirmishes since World War II. Trillions of dollars spent on weaponry. Our brightest minds have been devoted to developing ever more sophisticated weapons of mass destruction. Over 200,000 veterans of that war still suffer full-blown symptoms of traumatic stress, perhaps even more vividly than the more well known Vietnam vets.

It was an enormous feat to amass such a mighty war machine to overcome Germany and Japan. Rosie the Riveter went into the factories to turn out hundreds of thousands of airplanes, 90,000 tanks, 7 million rifles, 8 million bombs. The legacy? An abiding assumption that peace depends on an ongoing massive military buildup.

89

Living under the bomb reinforces and ultimately legitimates the epidemic of violence we face in our lives and our world, and deprives us of the precious resources to tackle poverty worldwide.

One of the prevailing myths of our time is that peace flows from the capacity, willingness and announced intention to eliminate our enemies. There is another way, the way of nonviolence and negotiation. To create such alternatives with all of the ardor we can muster is the number one priority of the world today.

17

Elders Learn New Wisdom

Spring 1992. Louie meets with a men's group discussing ways to break-down the myth's that lead to our ingrained patterns of warmaking.

Recently Pace e Bene sponsored a gathering of men who grew up in the fire and afterglow of World War II, to explore the meaning and mode of war making as reflected in this epic struggle. World War II continues to be the basic pattern for the U.S. in responding to global conflict. The script George Bush put into action in the Persian Gulf, was just that in which he had participated as a Navy pilot and decorated hero in WWII. Kennedy, Johnson, Nixon, Carter, and Reagan had done no differently. The group that gathered included veterans of the Second World War, a conscientious objector of that time, and those who were children then but grew up watching the films and idolizing the heroes.

What we reflected on was the myth that connects our noble goals of freedom, democracy, the American Dream, peace, national security, faithfulness to God, and even physical survival, to a script that brings the energy of the United States into the factories and onto the beaches of conflict—John Wayne's character, for example, dying a hero's death on the beaches of Iwo Jima. We saw that whenever our national well-being is threatened, and to some degree that of our friends and allies, we send the Fleet, the Air Armada, the Battalions of tanks and fighting men into the fray. We are noble men—warriors—who are ready to fight and willing to die for the noble goals of our country.

That afternoon, we began to question whether there is a connection. Are these fleets and armadas the best way or even an effective way to achieve victory? What did the war in the Persian

Gulf achieve? There was a great cost in lives and dollars, at least of the "enemy." But is the world freer, safer, and more democratic? At the same time, we have seen the undoing of one of the best-defended and most aggressive totalitarian forces in the history of the world, the Soviet Union, without the use of any of those mighty weapons. People power brought that regime to a quick and decisive end in a manner that still makes the world speechless. A new script is being written. Freedom, democracy, physical survival, the practice of religion, and peace are achieved, not with massive weapons, but with masses of people entering the streets. Tanks were stopped, not with smart weapons, but with smart people who talked with their brothers and sisters and invited them to join.

Yes, perhaps God is revealing to us a new way. We need a new myth in our land, no longer that of brave and well-armed soldiers hitting the beaches under the cover of massive barrages from the mightiest fleets and armadas ever seen, but of brave women and men who can stand up for justice nonviolently against evil and oppressive systems and win.

18

Jesus Weeps Over Los Angeles

This essay was written in 1992 after Rodney King was beaten by Los Angeles police officers and in the wake of the civil disturbance that took place in Los Angeles, California when these officers were originally exonerated.

The last of the U.S. Army troops have been ordered back to their home base. The curfews are lifted. The final fire has fizzled out. The cameras are pointed elsewhere. Now, the events of April begin to fade.

But, like the haunting after-image of a stark black-and-white photo that has seared the mind's eye, this event won't go away. The shock, rage, and sorrow that washed over Los Angeles and Las Vegas and elsewhere in the wake of the absurd verdict in the beating case of motorist Rodney King nags at us. The realities these events brought into focus seem so large and mysterious, yet also simple. There are hints that they somehow hold the key to the meaning of our culture, if only we have the modesty and courage to try the lock.

For some, these events are a call to action—a time to finally roll up our sleeves and deal with the crushing multitude of social and economic problems that create and sustain poverty, exclusion and racism. Community and church leaders are saying we must hear the need and answer with substantial economic and social programs. They are disturbed that there does not seem to be a national political will to do anything very much.

We might also consider it a call to compassion — that whatever action we take must be rooted in a profound spirituality of human encounter.

The Gospel states that Jesus "wept over Jerusalem." The people of Jesus' time suffered multiple oppressions from the occupying Roman army and from burdens placed on them by the Temple hierarchy. Jesus was greatly saddened at this condition that was contrary to the spirit of God. He must be equally saddened as he looks at the world today with its growing number of poor.

The events in Los Angeles have jolted many whites and others into seeing more clearly than ever the poverty and the systemic violence of injustice of their city. Los Angeles is a home to the very rich. But it is also a city of the very poor. Some have dubbed it "the first Third World city in the US." *The Los Angeles Times* recently noted that "globalization of Los Angeles has produced devastating poverty for those weak in skills and resources." The continual cry of the poor is for jobs. Yet in Los Angeles joblessness grows at an alarming rate. Statistics project unemployment for the next generation at 8-10%, with 40-50% for youth of color. It might even be worse. Presently, there is 70% unemployment in South Central Los Angeles. Moreover, there is little hope for new jobs because most of the old jobs are now being done by people outside the country.

The increasing joblessness is a cause of alarm to all working people in the area. We know the agony of people who have no money.

But it is not just new people that experience poverty. The community that survived the 1965 Watts uprising, for example, has slipped farther and farther into unrelieved poverty. Educational systems and social services have failed to lift people from housing projects into the mainstream. There are no ladders out. This is doubly frustrating in a society whose media incessantly projects the "American way of life" of expensive clothes, cars, and millions of other consumer goods. And so a new morality grows. One cannot help but have compassion for frustrated dreams and lives of the next generation.

It is easy to lay blame. Almost every political voice did so in the wake of the events in Los Angeles. Life chances — the world of opportunity — are very different depending on one's social and economic location. Living the past two decades in an African

American community in Las Vegas that has few resources, we see the consequence every day.

When Pope John Paul II visited the United States, Donna Hanson, a mother, was chosen to speak to him regarding the life of lay people. We were moved to hear her ask the Pope: "Will you walk in our shoes?" What a prophetic statement. This is the essence of compassion: "to suffer with." Will we walk in the shoes of mothers who often have nothing to feed their children and perhaps end up hitting a local store for diapers on a day that seemed to the poor like a day of dispensation? Do we recognize the plight of the frustrated black and Latino teenagers? If we stopped to listen to their music we would get the message. It is full of despair, frustration, anger and little hope, except perhaps for that distant voice that said "you can change things...by any means available." We have seen these youth, and sometimes their parents, thrown to the ground by the same police who mostly treat whites with respect. Maybe these officers are scared, too, but they have the power.

What has happened to us that we are so fearful of one another? Perhaps the policemen were really frightened of Rodney King. That seems hard to imagine, though the jurors thought so. It was wrong to hold the trial among people who could not understand Rodney King's experience, but why should the residents of Simi Valley be so frightened? The cycle of fear, though, does not end there. We also can imagine the despair of the Korean-Americans whose stores were literally wiped out by fire and looting. And then there is little Latasha, killed by a Korean store owner as she was about to pay for a bottle of juice. How far will we let the vicious circle of fear isolate and dehumanize us? Must our doorways be littered with bodies? Must our streets become rivers of blood, set against a ragged horizon of flames?

Are we paralyzed by the expectations that our society has set for us — that whites sympathize with a white driver dragged from his car and beaten, or African Americans empathize with the mother of Latasha, or with the angry youths who know police brutality and are

95

galled to see four white officers "get away with it one more time"? Are we caught in the trap of suffering with "our own" — or can we "suffer with" (have compassion for) those unlike ourselves? Can we suffer with the black youth, the poor Latina mother, the white driver or the Korean immigrant?

A distraught Rodney King made a desperate plea: "Can't we all get along?" A white woman reporter who covered the area of destruction during and after the inferno talked with many people from all sides. She saw abuses on every side. But she came away convinced that if we really get together, talk to each other, even argue with each other, but stay together, we can "get along."

But it will take a generous heart. And it will take structural change.

The growing gap between the affluent and the poor must be reversed. There are solutions. But it takes dollars — and the dollars will not be forthcoming until we create a moral and political climate dedicated to a fresh start. With that kind of will, we could scrap our military budget and use those resources to address poverty both here and in the poorest parts of the world. By exercising that kind of creative nonviolence, we would begin to realize that we do not need big armies abroad — or at home.

More than ever, we are committed to a process of deepening nonviolence — not only nonviolence as a tactic, but nonviolence as a way of life, as an art of life. This art of nonviolence offers us new choices not only when we are confronted by a conflict to resolve, but also changing our deepest reactions to other human beings, and to the rest of the natural world which cries out for an end to wholesale abuse and exploitation.

Let us work together for the needed changes in our culture which imposes its terrible destructiveness on so many people, both here at home and in many countries around the world. Let us together be a sign of the compassion and nonviolence of God who does not wish such a destructiveness in us. Let God's compassion dwell inside us and bear the fruit of nonviolence in us.

19

Dazzling Violence

December 1992. Pace e Bene welcomed John Kavanaugh to Cathedral Hall, just yards away from The Las Vegas Strip. The group gathered in the shadows of this glaring symbol of modern distraction to reflect, together, on the way back to the personal form of life of the gospel.

The Las Vegas Strip dazzles millions of visitors every year with its row of monumental casinos that erupt out of the Nevada desert in a rainbow of hypnotic neon. The Mirage, one of the city's many hotel and casino complexes, reinforces this sense of eruption by sporting an enormous volcano that thunders and spews fire every fifteen minutes.

The glitter of The Strip, in many ways, is the fulfillment of our consumer society. Preying on the human need for recreation, every technique of human motivation and stimulation is used to tempt people to spend their money. There is the bright stimulation of light and noise, of sexual seduction and erotic stimulation. There are subliminal messages that pump these drives deeply into one's psyche and result in emptying one's purse. Most recently, it has even come to light that new, suggestive odors have been pumped into casinos to lure people to gamble away forty percent more of their money.

Pace a Bene was founded to look at our way of life and to address the violence in our society. In looking at the violence of the world, we are stunned by the massive volume of weapons, by the violence of the street, and by domestic violence. But we are becoming increasingly aware of another form of pervasive violence—the violence of consumerism.

A major mentor for us in this understanding is the brilliant Jesuit philosopher, John Kavanaugh, whose widely acclaimed book *Following Christ in a Consumer Society: The Spirituality of Cultural Resistance*, first appeared in 1981 from Orbis Press.

In this volume, Kavanaugh contrasts the commodity form of life to the personal, that of the gospel. He shows from our own culture, especially in advertising, our total absorption in the things we buy. We have become the ultimate consumers. It becomes our identity, as suggested by the current bumper sticker, "I buy, therefore I am." Kavanaugh documents the violence that an affluent life lived by a relative few perpetrates on the poor of the world. Even more so, he illuminates for us the devastating effect of this consumerism on our own personhood. The life of peace and nonviolence invites us to reject this consumerism, share our resources with the poor, and live simply as we follow Jesus. This is a better way toward becoming our true selves and discovering peace.

20

Las Vegas Reflections

Fall 1993. Through the spectacle of a Las Vegas hotel demolition, Louie remarks on the contrast of this event and the deeper realities of life in Las Vegas, where poverty and the environment are an afterthought.

Las Vegas newspapers have long been accustomed to reporting explosions at the Nevada Test Site in terms of the impact at "ground zero." Presently there is a hard won moratorium on nuclear testing, but, recently the Las Vegas paper presented pictures of a thirty foot high stack of rubble at "ground zero" on the Las Vegas Strip.

The article referred to the deliberate destruction of the twenty-three floor Dunes Casino-Hotel that was loaded with dynamite and imploded within a matter of seconds. This dramatic staging was part of the grand opening festivities of Steve Wynn's new mega-casino, Treasure Island.

The Dunes tower was destroyed to clear ground for another Wynn mega-casino. Some three hundred and seventy-nine members of the media, including the major television networks, were on hand. Over 200,000 people poured into Las Vegas to witness the spectacular event. Explosives that were necessary for the collapse of the building were greatly enhanced by additional fireworks and conflagrations to thrill onlookers. Called one of the great celebrations of our times by civic officials and newscasters, this event will soon be the subject of an hour long TV movie acclaiming the joy and excitement of Las Vegas.

While many had fun coming to Las Vegas to watch such an affair, we must honestly question the deeper impact of such an event. Las Vegas continues to have a great shortage of affordable housing. A long awaited and promised shelter for homeless people still has not come into existence. Every winter homeless people and seniors freeze to death on the streets or in unheated quarters. In light of all of this, a modern hotel with 1,000 rooms is destroyed as an extravaganza.

Such incongruities continue as one views the strip with more critical eyes. The Mirage, Wynn's flagship casino, has been noted for its extravagance in display. Every fifteen minutes a volcano explodes and gives off a great fire and water show. It has been said that the amount of gas used for the explosion costs some $2,000 a shot. Increasingly, the new mega-casinos exploit the resources of water and power to create enormous displays to attract tourists. Can our earth continue this reckless use of limited resources?

The purchase of the Dunes was most desired for its water rights that can now be exploited for more of Wynn's extravaganzas. The result is a series of ecological nightmares. The waste of water, gas and power at Wynn's mega-casinos, and at other casinos, is astronomical. On one level the implosion of the Dunes can be seen as simply adding to the pollution of the Las Vegas atmosphere as onlookers hid from the fallout of the blast. On another level the implosion may symbolize the impending implosion of our culture if such activities continue. With this implosion there will be nowhere to hide.

At Pace e Bene we consider the waste of limited natural resources to be one of the major contributors to violence in the world. The picture of the fireball that consumed the hotel tower with the resultant twisted debris at "ground zero" might signal to us that once again the sacred desert is the scene of the destruction of our wonderful gift of creation. Francis's sense of reverence for all creation and love of the poor challenges us to look beyond the glitz of this "wild and wonderful event" and ponder the limited resources of our world and how we can better share them.

21

Sharing the Fruits of the Garden of Eden

Spring 1993. Louie reflects on the gifts of creation and how living according to our needs and not our wants allows these gifts to be shared by all.

Former United Nations Assistant Secretary General Robert Muller recently raised a clarion cry to those who follow the spirit and charism of Francis of Assisi. He noted that even the United Nations picks up on Francis's vision by its commitment to help the poor and downtrodden, to call for peace, disarmament and demilitarization, and to encourage cooperation between heads of states. Muller further stated that we have not addressed the bedrock of life: "simple and frugal living in order not to tax unduly God's marvelous creation." Alerting us that the United Nations is convoking a conference on population next year, he urged that a conference also be held on simple, frugal living.

Surely Muller's argument, noting that the citizenry of the rich world used thirty times the resources of those in the poor world, needs no great debate. It might be more convenient for those of us in the richer nations if the poor would limit their population and thus allow us, at least temporarily, to continue to over-consume our resources, as well as those that nature has given to people living in poorer parts of our world.

The recent war in Iraq, which was patently fueled by the desire for us to control Middle East oil resources while wasting our own, is only one example of how our desire for resources beyond our share is played out. It is inconvenient for us to give up our hardwood mantle-pieces when wood is needed to shelter, warm and feed children living in environments still occupied by indigenous people. Although we understand the crucial role that rainforests play in the global ecology, it feels like a distant reality when contrasted with our everyday lifestyle. Yet doesn't the beauty of old-growth rain forests cry out for preservation just for the sake of that beauty?

We do not like to hear words like "frugality." We have worked hard to develop so many enjoyable ways to consume the gifts of creation. Why should we deny ourselves now? The thought of frugal smacks of an older Puritan sparseness that we find out of keeping with "the abundant society." Taken to its Latin roots, however, "frugal" is derived from the word for "fruit." Frugality is associated with the fruitfulness and richness of the earth. Milton spoke of the world as "Nature, wise and frugal." At its essence, frugality speaks of enjoying the fruitfulness of the earth. Such appreciation of the created gift of fruit does not allow room for waste or abuse, which ultimately deprives us of the deep taste of the gifts of the sacredness of life.

22

Immigration and Nonviolence

Winter 1995. Louie writes about a California legislative bill harming immigrants; the roots of such a bill and how nonviolence could be used to counteract such legislation.

In the last election California passed Proposition 187 that would drastically restrict health and education services to anyone without documents entitling them to live in the United States. Shortly after the passage of Proposition 187, a twelve-year-old boy died of leukemia in Los Angeles because his mother was too frightened to take him to the hospital until it was too late. A week later, a seventy-six-year old Chinese woman in San Francisco, also suffering from leukemia, died because she too was afraid to go to the hospital until it was too late. When institutions incorporate restrictions on the basis of race or nationality, as in these cases, we have a clear case of systemic racism. The result of this institutional racism is a real violence to those affected.

In the paradigms of modem liberation struggles, this violence is termed *initiating violence*. The traditional response when this reaches a crisis is revolutionary violence. Indeed, some feel so victimized by such legislation and the effects of the resulting policies, especially on their families, that they yearn for revolution. Injustice does call for a response, as Gandhi insisted; but Gandhi would urge a response of nonviolence.

What form can this response take? First, one must make a good analysis. What is really going on to provide such a reaction? Is it because they are immigrants? Almost everyone who voted comes from immigrant stock, and for the most part from ethnic backgrounds that were themselves subject to such discrimination in California. Supporters of Proposition 187 insist the law addresses only illegal immigrants; but again a large portion of our immigrant ancestors also came without papers. The root cause seems to be that many in California feel an economic squeeze. Their actual earning power has eroded while a more sophisticated marketing economy has seduced them into enormous spending habits that leave them with decreasing incomes to cover their increasing bills. Whom do they blame? They focus on those who might work for less than they are willing to work for, thus threatening their employment. Even if they cannot find a direct connection between their economic ills and the immigrants, it is easier to project their insecurity on these powerless members of the lowest strata than to look toward those who have constructed the economic system to be highly profitable to the few. Yet this system means the destruction of both the working class—production occurs either abroad or in non-union sweatshops in the inner city—and of the middle class, who can be replaced by fewer and fewer technocrats who can do the work with computers.

Some years ago I read an article in *Forbes* by one of the Forbes 500 executives. He said, "Why don't we be honest and admit it. We control the turnstile at the border. When we want labor we loosen it, and when the labor market is too abundant we tighten it."

Where do we go from here? Gandhi insisted we have to identify the opponent, which in this case is the economic system controlled by large, profit oriented corporations. We are called to develop strategies that address the crippling injustice done to immigrants in this country. A statewide interfaith coalition is developing strategies to address the source of this injustice. Creative and nonviolent ideas are coming forth. We are convinced that with this momentum a new, more vital community will emerge, and our economy and our culture will be far richer.

PART FIVE

A NEW WORLD OF NONVIOLENCE

The greatest challenge of the day is: how to bring about a revolution of the heart, a revolution which has to start with each one of us?

— Dorothy Day

We can change the world if we do it nonviolently. If we can just show people how they can organize nonviolently, we can't fail. Nonviolence has never failed when it's tried.

— Cesar Chavez

To me, nonviolence is the all-important virtue to be nourished and studied and cultivated.

— Dorothy Day

Nonviolence is the greatest and most active force in the world. One person who can express nonviolence in life exercises a force superior to all the forces of brutality.

— Mahatma Gandhi

The choice is no longer violence or nonviolence. It's nonviolence or non-existence.

— Martin Luther King, Jr., April 3, 1968

We have to make truth and nonviolence not matters for mere individual practice but for practice by groups and communities and nations. That at any rate is my dream. I shall live and die in trying to realize it.

— Mahatma Gandhi

Another Kind of Power: Fr. Louie's Reflections on Nonviolence

Nonviolence is a force for transformation, justice, and the well-being of all that is neither violent nor passive. It is love in action (Dorothy Day), cooperative power (Jonathan Schell), and transforming power (Alternatives to Violence). As the War Resister's League puts it in both a broader and more detailed way, nonviolence "is an active form of resistance to systems of privilege and domination, a philosophy for liberation, an approach to movement building, a tactic of non-cooperation, and a practice we can employ to transform the world." Dr. Martin Luther King, Jr. succinctly calls it "the love that does justice."

Fr. Louie has been experimenting with each of these facets of nonviolence for over half a century. Through his words and deeds, he has explored how nonviolence is a stand for justice and a method for helping to create it. He has been activating what the late activist and writer Barbara Deming called "the two hands of nonviolence": noncooperation with injustice and steadfast regard for the opponent as a human being.

For Fr. Louie, nonviolence is the power of creative love in contrast to the power of fear, hate and greed. It is an orientation, a set of principles, a method, and specific strategies that put this power of love into practice. It is a way of life and a means of transforming the planet. It challenges the power of and belief in violence and its destructiveness geared toward threatening, dominating, or defeating others.

Nonviolence—palpably evident in Fr. Louie's journey—offers an antidote to this destruction by unleashing the ingredients of a more human way: compassion, connection, creativity, and profound communion with all the world.

Louie's intuition about the power of nonviolence has been increasingly corroborated worldwide. In spite of widely held assumptions that nonviolence is ineffective, people around the planet go on building one nonviolent people-power movement after another. Rather than being held back by pervasive beliefs about nonviolence as otherworldly and unrealistic, they act as if the vision, strategies, and tools of nonviolent change are transformative and effective. We are consequently awash in a growing proliferation of nonviolent campaigns building more democratic societies, championing human rights, struggling for economic justice, and working to safeguard the planet. As detailed in historian Jonathan Schell's book, The Unconquerable World: Power, Nonviolence and the Will of the People (2003), organizing nonviolent people power for liberation and human rights has emerged and increased over the past 300 years. Beginning in the twentieth century this momentum accelerated with Mohandas Gandhi's application of principled nonviolence to win Indian independence and with the use of disciplined nonviolence by the U.S. Civil Rights Movement.

These and other pioneering campaigns have inspired countless nonviolent struggles. Some examples include successful pro-democracy movements in Spain and Portugal (1970s), the Philippines (1986), Chile (1980s), Argentina (1980s), Soviet bloc states, including the Velvet Revolution in Czechoslovakia, Poland, East Germany, etc. (1989); the thwarted coup in the USSR (1991); South Africa (1980s-1990s); Indonesia (1998); East Timor (2000); Serbia (2000); Georgia (2003); Ukraine (2004); Liberia (2005); and Tunisia and Egypt (2011). These are not isolated cases; a recent book by Erica Chenoweth and Maria J. Stephan called Why Civil Resistance Works analyzed 323 major social struggles across the globe between 1900 and 2006 and concluded that nonviolent campaigns have been twice as successful as violent ones.

Increasingly Fr. Louie's belief that nonviolence works has been underscored by real world practice.

The following essays offer glimmers of this faith in the power of nonviolence to transform our lives, our societies, and our world. They include a loving reflection on his friend and colleague, Cesar Chavez—the co-founder of the United Farm Workers—at the time of his passing in 1993; an exploration of the potential for nonviolence in our time; and, finally, a review of James Douglass's ground-breaking book, The Nonviolent Coming of God. Together, these chapters offer Fr. Louie's clear testimony to the power and potential of nonviolence in our time.

23

Cesar Chavez: A Prophet of Nonviolence

Summer 1993. Louie reflects on his time at Cesar Chavez's funeral, remembering Chavez's commitment to nonviolence while working for the farm workers basic human rights.

Some fifty thousand mourners descended upon Delano, California for the funeral of Cesar Chavez, who died in April 1993. Thousands of others gathered in many other places to commemorate this great leader. The response to his passing could not but leave a great impression, for Cesar's life made a very deep mark on our current era. What is the legacy passed on by this hero of our times? The tributes came from President Bill Clinton, Jesse Jackson, the Kennedy family, and Cardinal Roger Mahony, who celebrated the funeral. Dolores Huerta, the co-founder with Chavez of the United Farm Workers, and Cesar's own sons and the new emerging leadership of the UFW, all spoke of the impact of Cesar's charisma on their lives and on our times.

Chavez's life and work always reflected the fact that he was first and foremost a farmworker who spoke from the point of view of a very oppressed working group who put food on the table of a very affluent nation. Cesar was an organizer, founding a union of the migrant poor that won the respect and active support of big labor. Hispanics hail him as the one who gave them dignity and respect in the land of their origins where they had been excluded from their entitlements. Church spokespersons acclaim Cesar as a prophet, one who told it like it was on behalf of God's oppressed peoples.

At Pace e Bene we remember him especially as one of the major proponents of nonviolence in our time. At Cesar's funeral Jesse Jackson ranked Cesar together with Martin Luther King, Jr., calling them the great advocates and activists of nonviolence in the history of this country. Like King, Chavez was a student and follower of Gandhi.

A close rapport had grown between these two men towards the end of Martin's life. I had the opportunity to be present at a small commemoration service that Cesar called in Delano the night of King's assassination. At the time, Cesar expressed feelings of deep connection with King and a terrible sense of loss at his death.

Cesar held with Gandhi that "nonviolence is not passivity in any shape or form. Nonviolence is the most active force in the world." At King's death Chavez wrote to his widow: "His nonviolence was that of action—not that of one contemplating action. Because of that, he will always be to us more than a philosopher of nonviolence. Rather, he will be remembered by us as a man of peace." Cesar insisted, "We must respect all human life, in the cities and in the fields and in Vietnam. Nonviolence is the only weapon that is compassionate and recognizes each person's value."

But Cesar described nonviolence for his movement as "aggressive nonviolence." Militant nonviolence is our means for social revolution and to achieve justice for our people."

Perhaps most notable in Cesar Chavez' pursuit of nonviolence was the practice of fasting. Like Gandhi, fasting was a form of purification, and a means of overcoming violence, including within his own movement and within his own soul. At the end of a twenty-one day fast in 1968 he said, "I am not completely nonviolent yet, and I know it. That is why I fasted; I felt it was a very personal form of self-testing and of prayer. Anyone could be nonviolent in a monastery... What's difficult is to be nonviolent in the cause, in the battle for social justice."

I recall Cesar sharing his thoughts on that fast not long after it ended. He traveled at great personal cost to be with a small group of us who were fasting to express our concern about the war in

Vietnam. His sharing of the deep significance of fasting left a lasting impression on me.

Above all, Cesar was a man of intense faith and religious belief. A number of Franciscan Friars who knew him throughout the years were always deeply impressed with his devotion. It was on the occasion of one visit during a community celebration that he arrived at the idea of making a march to the state capitol at Sacramento a religious procession under the banner of Our Lady of Guadalupe. His nonviolence rested in a deep faith that God can bring about powerful transformation.

Cesar was clear that nonviolence is the way of God. This way included for him a deep respect for all living beings, including animals, and was manifest in his staunch vegetarianism. For him, it was not compatible to eat meat and be in pursuit of nonviolence.

Cesar knew that many "more worldly minded unionists" would leave the union effort, but he was confident that his own people would stay. Seeing the tens of thousands of people pour into Delano through the night vigil before his funeral was witness to this testimony. He has been a major inspiration and teacher of nonviolence for me and for many others. It is my hope that we can continue to plumb the deep richness of his nonviolence as a guide to social transformation in the spirit of the God of nonviolence.

24

Nonviolence Comes of Age

Fall 1997. Louie writes on new technologies in the home and in warfare, but he also notices a new movement for nonviolence coming into the fore.

Numerous expectations for the new millennium are on the horizon. Many of them tout new technologies. Bill Gates just finished building his new $50 million dollar home. Among its gadgets are pins that each person in the house wears to acclimatize the room and adjust the music as the wearer enters. We have new ventures in outer space with little rovers wandering on distant planets. Under the guise of *Stockpile Weapons Stewardship* are new ventures in the development of nuclear weapons: the "National Ignition Facility," under construction in Livermore, CA costing $1.3 billion, and the "Sub-Critical Tests," at the Nevada Test Site last June and September. Veterans from the early development of nuclear weapons warn us that we are entering into a new age of nuclear weapons development. One day it may be possible that, without the need to acquire enriched uranium, a 65 megaton bomb could be built by almost any nation. Taken in a van and parked in a major city, it could blow the city from the face of the world.

On the other end of the scale, something even more powerful is emerging – a growing acceptance around the world of nonviolence.

The best modern expression of nonviolence emerged with Mahatma Gandhi, Dr. Martin Luther King, Jr., and the Civil Rights Movement popularized in the United States. Subsequently, such practitioners as Cesar Chavez, Dorothy Day, the Berrigan Brothers, and others throughout the world extended its visibility and practice. Though these movements seem to suddenly rise up independently, they have had a long tradition and an ongoing connection and development. When Pace e Bene was founded almost ten years ago, Alain Richard stated that if this was truly a new age of nonviolence, we would see signs of nonviolence springing up all over the world. This is surely happening today. In much of Latin America, South Africa, the Philippines and other parts of Asia, we have seen the almost unbelievable and unpredictable transformation of nations from repressive dictatorships by means of nonviolence.

It was interesting to hear recent congressional criticism of the Central Intelligence Agency for its failure to predict the radical transformation of Eastern Europe and the former Soviet Union. Its spy system seemed able only to monitor and predict military coups. Some congresspersons suggested that perhaps the C.I.A. had outlived its times. Our hypothesis about the coming age of nonviolence might support that conclusion. The lessons are not forgotten. Recently when it looked as though the Philippine president might declare martial law or override the constitution, Cardinal Sin and other church and community leaders promoted a rally of thousands to prevent such action before it began. There are now thousands of grassroots movements of nonviolence around the world.

Not only have nonviolent movements been successful in the face of the mightiest military machines ever created, but we see more and more efforts to transform local communities through nonviolence. Cities such as Santa Maria and Santa Rosa in California and Silver City in New Mexico, for instance, have *Nonviolence Days* to recreate their towns through projects of nonviolence. Recently twenty Nobel Peace Prize Laureates signed a statement calling The United Nations to declare the year 2000 *The Year for Nonviolence* and to declare the decade 2000-2010, *A Decade for a Culture of Peace and Nonviolence.*

Pace e Bene is trying to connect nonviolence to every aspect of the culture. From its founding, Pace e Bene has focused on cultural transformation realizing that a major source of violence is the culture. For example, our highly consumerized culture wreaks violence on provider nations, on low skilled workers, and on consumers themselves.

Consumer boycotts have become more common. Recently boycotts have been directed at manufacturers such as Nike for their exploitation of workers, including children, in parts of Asia. Cesar Chavez pointed out that if 7% of the population boycotts a product, the company will be forced to negotiate a change in policy. We are also noting that nonviolence is more and more utilized to protect our environment, especially as it is impacted by extreme consumerism. Again consumer boycotts are most effective. The recent nonviolent occupation of the headwaters in Northern California has been effective in protecting old growth redwoods. *Critical Mass organizes monthly "bike actions" in which thousands of bicycles flood the streets of urban America.* In San Francisco I participate with *Religious Witness with Homeless People* as we work to make housing on an abandoned military base available to those without shelter. In Nevada, resistance continues at the Nevada Test Site. These are just a few examples; surely you can add countless examples from your own region.

Growth in nonviolence education is as impressive as growth in nonviolent action. Major universities now offer degrees in *Peace Studies* that include courses such as *Conflict Resolution, Mediation, Nonviolent Direct Action,* and *Civil Disobedience.* Training in nonviolence for direct action is becoming part of the necessary education for life in these times. Ken Butigan and I are amazed by the numbers who enroll for our annual class, *The Spirituality of Nonviolence,* each spring at the Franciscan School of Theology in Berkeley, California.

Theologian and activist James Douglass holds that Jesus came into the world to bring about a transformation from a society of violence and domination to a community of compassion and sharing. When he called his followers to take up the cross and follow him, he meant assuming the nonviolent posture of accepting personal suffering rather than imposing it on one's sisters and brothers. Two millennia later, Gandhi recognized the radical transformation this would bring. It remains the formula for the emergence of the new creation, the reign of God.

Is this the time? Are we beginning to see the dawning of "the coming of the nonviolent God?" We live in hope. May we struggle to welcome God's new world of nonviolence.

25

The Nonviolent Coming of God

Summer 1992. Louie reflects on the book "The Nonviolent Coming of God" by James Douglass as a relevant thesis for nonviolent social change in our time.

Many have acclaimed theologian and activist James Douglass as the foremost prophet of nonviolence in our country today. In the aftermath of the verdict in the beating case of Los Angeles motorist Rodney King we are aware that we need a true solution to the injustices that so many experience in this country and in the world. Yet we likewise abhor the violence that followed the decision, and look for a way to change, without destroying our communities. What can we do? Douglass persuasively maintains, with his life and with his words, that the way which has been tried and proven by Gandhi, Martin Luther King, Jr., Dorothy Day and Cesar Chavez — the way of active nonviolence can show us how to resolve this dilemma and lead to a new culture of peace.

In his magnificent book, *The Nonviolent Coming of God*, Douglass documents how this is the way of Jesus. Jesus lived at a time of enormous oppression. His land was an occupied territory controlled by the repressive Roman empire, which ultimately put him to death. At the same time the poor were burdened by the oppressive Temple economy organized and enforced by the religious establishment. Jesus foresaw an impending violent insurrection sparked by this political and economic oppression. Such a war of liberation would, in turn, lead to the Roman annihilation of Jerusalem. However, Douglass writes, "far from announcing Jerusalem's destruction as inevitable, Jesus' whole public life was an effort to create a radically alternative Jewish society. The nonviolent coming of God in that society would, he hoped, transform the violence of Rome, Palestine and the world."

In the Sermon on the Mount, Jesus explained the way of active nonviolence: love your enemies, turn the other cheek, offer nonviolent resistance to one who does evil, seek first the Kingdom of God. Moreover, he taught this wisdom of nonviolent action by example. He stopped the big business in the Temple as a nonviolent response to the oppression done to the poor.

Douglass' thesis is that Jesus called on the people of his time neither to submit apathetically and powerlessly to the status quo, nor to use counter-violence as a means of change, but instead to unleash a creative, redemptive, active love to welcome God's reign of nonviolence. But the people did not listen. They did not follow him by taking up the cross and turning violence into love. Instead, from 66-70 C.E., an armed uprising designed to liberate the country convulsed the nation and, in turn, Roman might decimated Jerusalem and reinforced its occupation.

For Douglass, this reading of the New Testament has enduring implications for our own day. Jerusalem has become the world, he says. He urges us to use the nonviolent ways of God announced by Jesus to transform the inequities and oppression in the world today. Echoing the famous dictum of Martin Luther King, Douglass concludes, "Our choice is between nonviolence and nonexistence."

Knowing that more and more nations are building nuclear weapons while our own massively armed nuclear submarines prowl the world's seas sharpens King's and Douglass's stark choice. There is a powerful, nonviolent way forward, but it means addressing the pain and injustice of our world. If we are willing to take up our cross and organize movements of nonviolence, we can welcome God's reign of peace.

Afterword

By John Dear

Fr. Louie Vitale is such an inspiration. I'm grateful to Ken Butigan and Pace e Bene for gathering together some of Louie's writings on peace and nonviolence so that others can learn from him and be inspired to join his campaign of nonviolence.

Here in this little collection, we've read Louie's reflections on St. Francis; heard Louie's call to serve the poor, end war, abolish nuclear weapons, and protect creation; caught a glimpse of his experience in jail for peacemaking; and been summoned to follow Jesus along the way of Gospel nonviolence. Louie's writings, like his life, invite us to join the struggle and dedicate ourselves to the great cause of justice, disarmament, peace and environmental sustainability.

Louie Vitale's lifelong work for justice and peace has touched thousands of people—from his work among the Franciscans, the farm workers, the poor of San Francisco to the thousands arrested at the Nevada Test Site, the thousands who have learned nonviolence from Pace e Bene, the peace group he helped found, and the thousands more who have been touched by his personal witness. He is, for many of us, the epitome of the Franciscan ideal, the embodiment of action which Pope Francis calls for, and a model Christian, a true peacemaker.

I've known Louie Vitale for almost thirty years, and I've seen his steadfast commitment to peace and nonviolence time and time again. His passion, free spirit, constant questioning, great dreams and visions, simplicity, humility, humor and friendship are a great blessing and consolation for many of us. Over the years, I've spoken along with him at various events, tried to support him during his stints in jail, and been arrested with him at various peace protests in California, Nevada and Georgia. I even journeyed with him to Cairo, Egypt, for the Gaza Freedom

March, the year before the Arab Spring broke out. For many of us, he makes life worth living.

One hilarious episode stands out. A few years ago in the Las Vegas, Nevada, Courthouse, fourteen of us stood trial for trespassing at Creech Air Force Base, the U.S. headquarters of its evil drone program. It was the first ever demonstration against U.S. drone warfare. We had worked hard to prepare for trial, and to speak out for an end to the U.S. drone attacks on Afghanistan. Former Attorney General Ramsey Clark agreed to testify on our behalf. When the day came, the courtroom was packed. The prosecutor stood up and denounced us as unpatriotic criminals who deserved to be harshly punished. He was furious, and the judge let him drone on and on.

Because this was not a jury trial, the guards put the fourteen of us in the jury box, and added two extra chairs at the end. Louie and I sat in these extra chairs. As the prosecutor carried on his bitter denunciations, Louie did something that shocked everyone. He fell asleep. Then, he started snoring!

Here we were, in court, on trial, facing a year in prison, being denounced by the prosecutor right in front of the judge, and this tall, skinny Franciscan is snoring away loudly—right in the middle of the prosecutor's angry speech. People started looking at one another and then the whole courtroom broke out laughing. I tried to wake him up, but he kept right on sleeping and snoring. Finally, the prosecutor gave up and sat down.

Here, I thought, is an entirely new Franciscan strategy of creative nonviolent resistance—fall asleep and snore in the face of federal prosecution. Eventually, we received time served, but none of us will never forget Louie's nonviolent witness that day in court.

Louie Vitale makes peacemaking a joyous adventure, even as he addresses the most serious issues of the day. "We are in a struggle for survival," he writes. "At this moment in history we must choose. If we continue to exploit our planet, it will be destroyed. This means the end of human life, but also of the magnificent creation that has reflected God's presence for billions of years. That is a great tragedy and sin. But it is not too late. If we can come to love creation, to cherish and care for it, we can find solutions."

Louie invites us to choose—to consciously side with creation, with the poor, and with God. He wants us to say "No to injustice and Yes to love in action." "We have to say No to violence, war and environmental destruction," he writes. "We have to end our exploitation and domination of the earth and the poor. At the same time, we have to say Yes to life, solidarity, conservation, dialogue and self-determination. We say Yes to creation and all her creatures. From now on, we strive to walk like St. Francis by treating all creation and all creatures with respect and love as our sisters and brothers."

Like Gandhi, Dr. King, Dorothy Day, and Cesar Chavez, Louie knows that this choice for justice and peace requires steadfast nonviolence. He calls us to practice nonviolence toward everyone and all creation. As we practice nonviolence, he says, we will discover anew our dependence on God, and God's abiding presence in our lives. We will realize that we no longer need weapons of war because now we place all our hope and trust in the God of peace. Through our creative nonviolence, we begin to recognize every human being as our sister and brother, and the presence of God in everyone and in creation itself.

"The transforming power of nonviolence begins and ends with an awareness of the presence of God in everyone," he writes. As we recognize God in others and in creation, we find the strength and courage to take bold steps to welcome God's nonviolent reign of peace on earth.

For Louie, the choice to work for justice and peace requires joining and working for the grassroots movement of nonviolence for the abolition of poverty, war, nuclear weapons and environmental destruction. "People around the planet go on building one nonviolent people power movement after another," he writes. "Rather than being held back by pervasive beliefs about nonviolence as otherworldly and unrealistic, they act as if the vision, strategies and tools of nonviolent change are transformative and effective. We are consequently awash in a growing proliferation of nonviolent campaigns building more democratic societies, championing human rights, struggling for economic justice and working to safeguard the planet."

"We need a new myth in our land," he continues, "no longer that of brave, well-armed soldiers hitting the beaches under the cover of massive barrages from the mightiest fleets and armadas ever seen, but of brave women and men who can stand up for justice nonviolently against evil and oppressive systems and win."

"Nonviolence works," Louie Vitale insists. "This must be our new myth, our new story."

In September, 2015, for the second year in a row, Pace e Bene organized a week of action called "Campaign Nonviolence." Thousands of people took part in over 370 demonstrations, marches and events in all fifty states calling for an end to poverty, war, racism, nuclear weapons and environmental destruction and for a new culture of peace and nonviolence. We were trying to connect the dots between all the issues of violence and help the various movements come together under the call for a new culture of peace and nonviolence. We hope to continue this great mobilization for years to come. (For a detailed list of events, and to join Campaign Nonviolence, visit www.campaignnonviolence.org.)

This is the kind of peacework that Louie has advocated all his life. He knows that the only way positive social change ever happens is through bottom up grassroots nonviolent movements, from Jesus and St. Francis to Gandhi and Martin Luther King, Jr. Throughout these pages, I hear Louie inviting all of us to get involved, take a stand, march in the streets, speak out, and pursue a more nonviolent world. What's more, he wants us to stay involved, like him, for the rest of our lives.

But like St. Francis, Fr. Louie Vitale also wants us to pursue justice and disarmament in a spirit of universal love. That spirit of love, he shows us, makes all the difference.

One night a few years ago, he called me from prison. "I've had a profound realization," he said excitedly. "Love is all that matters. All we have to do is love everyone from now on!"

It's such a simple insight, but one we need to learn over and over again, especially those of us who work for justice and peace. Louie Vitale says we can make a difference in the world, we can help end war, poverty, nuclear weapons and environmental destruction, we can welcome God's reign of peace, we can follow the nonviolent Jesus on the road to peace, but even more, we can do all that in a spirit of hope and joy because we love everyone. From now on, we practice unconditional, nonviolent, universal love.

For Fr. Louie Vitale, peacemaking, nonviolence and the struggle for justice are the normal signs of universal love, and after all is said and done, love is what matters.

What a blessing! Thank you, Fr. Louie.

Pace e Bene / Peace and Goodness

*Together we can imagine, create, and live a different way
and a different world*

Pace e Bene Nonviolence Service explores ways to tap the power of peace and goodness to make a difference in our lives, our communities, and our world through:

Nonviolent Education

Pace e Bene's nonviolent workshops, trainings, and study groups
provide concrete ways to grapple with the challenges we face and to inspire effective action. Pace e Bene has led over 800 workshops worldwide on the power of creative nonviolence to transform relationships and to engage societies.

Pace e Bene's publications, website, and speaking events
increase awareness of the core values and methods of creative nonviolence to discover positive alternatives to violence and passivity and to support the emergence of a culture of nonviolent options.

Nonviolent Community

Pace e Bene's growing network
supports individuals and organizations applying nonviolent methods for personal and social transformation. Pace e Bene seeks to promote the growth of nonviolent communities and the emergence of a nonviolent culture.

Nonviolent Action

Pace e Bene's programs offer individuals and organizations a process for taking concrete steps for nonviolent change.
Pace e Bene collaborates with organizations and movements that challenge the cycle of violence; foster just and lasting peace; champion human rights; confront the violence of poverty and all forms of oppression; and strengthen spiritually-based initiatives for a better world. In 2014 they launched Campaign Nonviolence a long-term movement to build a culture of peace and nonviolence free from war, poverty, the climate crisis, and the epidemic of violence.

www.paceebene.org

Campaign Nonviolence

A national grassroots movement to build a culture of peace and mainstream nonviolence, www.CampaignNonviolence.org.

Campaign Nonviolence is a new national grassroots movement that seeks to mobilize the nation and the world through the power of active nonviolence to help abolish war, poverty, environmental destruction and the epidemic of violence and build a new culture of peace and nonviolence. It seeks a culture that values, promotes, teaches, and applies the power of nonviolent transformation in the face of violence and injustice. It endeavors to take active nonviolence into the mainstream, and challenge the false notion that nonviolence is passive, weak, and ineffective. It works to make the tools of nonviolent transformation accessible to all. It wants to educate every human being in the method, way and wisdom of active nonviolence that one day, war will end, and everyone will live in peace with justice.

Campaign Nonviolence tries to spread the vision, principles and methods of active, creative nonviolence, even as it connects the dots between war, poverty, the climate crisis, and the epidemic of violence. No one of these monumental challenges will be solved separately. They are intimately connected and must be solved in an integral fashion. That's why Campaign Nonviolence invites us not only to connect the dots between the issues, but also to connect the dots between the organizations and movements that have been toiling separately for years for a better world. Campaign Nonviolence envisions an emerging "movement of movements" that joins forces, pools people-power, and works collaboratively in comprehensively addressing these challenges.

But there is more. Campaign Nonviolence insists that resolving these monumental challenges will only happen by unleashing the power of active, creative, liberating and audacious nonviolence. Nonviolence challenges the power and systems of violence through grassroots, bottom up, people power. It disarms, heals, rebuilds, and leads to a more just, more peaceful world, and it does so through just, peaceful means.

We organize marches and public actions for peace, justice and nonviolence each year during the third week of September, around International Peace Day, September 21st, as well as hold nonviolence trainings around the nation and promote "Nonviolent Cities."

Campaign Nonviolence calls upon people everywhere to join together in a new grassroots movement against war, poverty, the climate crisis and the epidemic of violence. We call upon Campaign Nonviolence people to practice nonviolence toward themselves, toward all others, and toward the planet, as we reenergize and rebuild a new global grassroots movement of nonviolence for a new world of peace. Together, we can make a difference, and do our part to make a new nonviolent world a reality.

www.CampaignNonviolence.org

Other Books from Pace e Bene Press

Engage

Exploring Nonviolent Living

A program for learning, practicing and experimenting with nonviolent options for our lives and for a sustainable, just and peaceful world

We have more power than we think.
Engage can help us tap into that power and equip us to improve our lives, our communities, and our world. Using numerous stories, exercises and resources, The *Engage* Workbook offers us a way to learn, study and practice the nonviolent options available to us. *Engage* provides tools for individuals and groups to take action for justice and peace in the midst of war and injustice. *Engage* is ideal for advocacy organization, campus networks, faith communities, and any group seeking to work together to create a society committed to justice, democracy, peace, sustainability and equality.

Engage, a project of Pace e Bene Nonviolence Service is based on the experience of leading hundreds of workshops. Order a copy of our book, *Engage: Exploring Nonviolent Living*, by Laura Slattery, Ken Butigan, Veronica Pelicaric and Ken Preston at www.paceebene.org.

The Nonviolent Life

A new book on
peacemaking

By John Dear

From Pace e Bene Press
to help build
Campaign Nonviolence

"How can we become people of nonviolence and help the world become more nonviolent? What does it mean to be a person of active nonviolence? How can we help build a global grassroots movement of nonviolence to disarm the world, relieve unjust human suffering, make a more just society and protect creation and all creatures? What is a nonviolent life?"

These are the questions John Dear—Nobel Peace Prize nominee, long time peace activist and Pace e Bene staff member—poses in this ground-breaking book. John Dear suggests that the life of nonviolence requires three simultaneous attributes: being nonviolent toward ourselves; being nonviolent to all people, all creatures, and all creation; and joining the global grassroots movement of nonviolence.

After thirty years of preaching the Gospel of nonviolence, John Dear offers a simple, original yet profound way to capture the crucial elements of nonviolent living, and the possibility of creating a new nonviolent world. According to John, "Most people pick one or two of these dimensions, but few do all three. To become a fully rounded, three dimensional person of nonviolence, we need to do all three simultaneously." Perhaps then he suggests, we can join the pantheon of peacemakers from Jesus and Francis to Dorothy Day and Mahatma Gandhi.

In this book, John Dear proposes a simple vision of nonviolence that everyone can aspire to. It will help everyone be healed of violence, and inspire us to transform our culture of violence into a new world of nonviolence! Order your copy at www.paceebene.org.

Biographies

Louie Vitale, OFM is a Franciscan priest who has sought to put the vision of peacemaking articulated and practiced by Francis and Clare of Assisi into practice. A former provincial of the St. Barbara Province in the western United States, Vitale was a co-founder of the Nevada Desert Experience—a spiritually-based movement that sought to end nuclear weapons testing at the Nevada Test Site—and Pace e Bene Nonviolence Service. As a long-time social activist, he has engaged in civil disobedience for nearly four decades in pursuit of peace and justice, and has been arrested more than 400 times.

Martin Sheen is an American actor and a long time peace and justice activist. He has been featured in "Apocalypse Now," "Gandhi" "Selma," and "The American President," as well as starred in TV's "The West Wing," and has campaigned against nuclear weapons and for workers' rights and many other causes. Sheen has been arrested numerous times during political demonstrations and protests.

John Dear is a priest, peace activist, lecturer and the author/editor of 30 books, including "The Nonviolent Life," "Jesus the Rebel," "The God of Peace," and "Thomas Merton Peacemaker." He has organized and participated in nonviolent campaigns for over three decades; been arrested some 75 times in acts of civil disobedience against war and injustice; and spent nearly a year of his life in jail for peace. He is on the staff of Pace e Bene and helps organize Campaign Nonviolence. www.johndear.org

Ken Butigan has spent many years working for a more just, peaceful and sustainable world. He is the director of Pace e Bene and a professor at DePaul University. His books include *Pilgrimage Through a Burning World: Spiritual Practice and Nonviolent Protest at the Nevada Test Site.*

To order copies of *Love is What Matters*:
Contact Pace e Bene Nonviolence Service
Phone: 510-268-8765
Email: info@paceebene.org
Website: www.paceebene.org

128